No Place for a Lady

Thea Rosenbaum

authorHOUSE®

AuthorHouse™ LLC
1663 Liberty Drive
Bloomington, IN 47403
www.authorhouse.com
Phone: 1-800-839-8640

Published by AuthorHouse 02/10/2014

ISBN: 978-1-4918-5705
ISBN: 978-1-4918-5704
ISBN: 978-1-4918-5703-8 (e)

Library of Congress Control Number: 2014901674

Table of Contents

Dedication

This book is dedicated to my children Peter and Petra,
who have been loving and patient with their mother. Also to
Gary who left us too early and who's unwavering early support

I will not forget.

Acknowledgment

I want to thank Chris Moore for putting my voice into words.
You always believed that we have a good story. And
I thank Jane Wittman-Roll for a terrific editing
job and constant positive suggestions.

Kathy Vandenberg took over the unwavering support
after her husband passed away; you are a beautiful person.

Thank you Irmgard Ross for believing early on in the book
and supporting it. I also want to thank my children, Peter
and Petra. Peter for keeping my feet firmly on the ground and
Petra for not hesitating to criticize when there was something to
criticize and to help her technically challenged mother. I know
how busy you are, yet you came through for me every time.

Introduction

While my mother and I were hiding from Russian soldiers in the ruins of Berlin in 1945, my cousin Helmut was escaping East Prussia on the last German train to the West. Behind them, the soldiers on board blew out the bridges to slow the advancing Soviets.

Helmut slept on the coal car, huddled together with another man for warmth. His family was lucky enough to sleep inside. Other Germans who went by foot froze to death, or starved, or were shot, or were strafed from the sky; and if they took to the sea they were torpedoed and drowned in the frozen Baltic. But Helmut and his family survived, as my family and I also survived. My father one day appeared in his uniform several months after the war ended. And then life began again.

Much of my family came from East Prussia, a place that no longer exists. I hadn't thought much of any of this for many years. I was focused on my career, first as Germany's only female stock broker, then in reporting on the Vietnam War or its aftermath; or in creating programs for German television in Washington D.C. for 30 years, and organizing European correspondents as a White House pool producer.

But when my mother died in 2008 shortly after my husband Jens passed the year before, I tracked down family members I had not seen or heard from in years to inform them of her death. In so doing, I became focused on my past and on my family's history in a way I had never been before.

What struck me about our story was how disconnected we had become from our family. In the good old days this was not true. And so I sought some way to at least, in part, fix our own family's separation by writing out our story. I believed we could all be reconnected by our own common history if only it were written down.

My cousin is an archeologist. We decided to write the story together. But then I began to have greater questions about myself. In particular I wanted to know in what ways my ancestors had shaped me. The East Prussians were known to be stubborn, tenacious go-getters. They were all hardy people and survivors. As I investigated my own past and ancestral heritage further, I was forced to relive so many of the things that I survived that I wanted to sort out the threads of my life and to write them down as my own story.

When I left for the United States with my husband Dick in the 1960s, my cousin Helmut stood beside me on a train platform in Bremen, Germany. We had just left a family get-together. He was immigrating to Canada.

He turned to me and said: "You are going to the United States. I am going to Canada. Let's see who becomes a millionaire first."

I thought it was an arrogant thing to say, but in recent years I found out that this was just his Prussian humor. In fact, he did become a millionaire. But I lived to tell as many stories, which over time are just as important for people as money. We connect through stories. It's how we see the larger picture; it's how we understand. And in my long career as a journalist and producer I lived through more than just interesting anecdotes for the nightly news. I personally got to see and experience the beginning and end of great historical stories that affected both my life and the lives of millions, like the creation of the Berlin Wall and its fall, or the Vietnam War and its aftermath.

In between these major bookends of war and freedom I saw and reported or produced stories that amazed me. In many ways I was amazed because I had never believed I would be successful in life. The horrors of my childhood made me think that I was ugly and stupid, and that I was only cut out to do what I was told. But as a reporter I didn't have to do what I was told; and as a producer, I was the one who did the telling. And so I found in my own life a real story that spans the later half of the 20th century and is personally entwined with its currents.

It tells an American story through German eyes, and a German story through American eyes. In Vietnam I saw the Vietnamese through the eyes of the conquered. I later saw American presidents both from a European perspective and as the mother of American children. But more than anything I saw life big and small. I was there when the KKK burned a school bus in Alabama, and I was there when the Vietcong tied five boys together in a rice paddy with one machine gun and forced them to slow advancing American soldiers. I screamed and held tight to my mother as a Byelorussian Soviet soldier tried to tear us apart to rape her. I've seen Hugh Heffner in his infamous bathrobe and reported on his Bunnies and their training. I've even been through Clown College at Ringling Brothers Barnum & Bailey Circus. What I've seen marks just a passing moment in time. But I think it marks it well. And I hope that this book might help someone, whether or not they are in my family, feel less disconnected than I had to feel.

Chapter 1

Khe-Sanh

I'm headed to Khe-Sanh in the jump seat of a C-130. Three weeks ago we didn't even know this place existed. It was just an out-of-the-way Marine base in the mountains near the North Vietnamese boarder. But since the North Vietnamese Army started to attack the Americans on the night of January the 21st, and landed a big hit, destroying the base's ammo dump, every journalist in Southeast Asia is trying to get here. The powers that be are allowing in only two journalists at a time for three-day clips. I'm lucky enough to be one of them, but I'm apprehensive as well. There's talk that Khe-Sanh will be the location of the largest battle in Vietnam. I'm only comforted because we think the military let a woman in since they were anticipating a lull in hostilities for the upcoming Tet holiday.

It's January 29th, 1968, and I'm glued to a jump seat behind the pilot, looking down on the approaching base. From above it's like a series of linked, reddish mud-bogs. Everything seems covered in dirt, the men included, an impression I confirm a little later. Outside the base are the hills and mountains, which are heavily fought over. From those hilltops, and other locations, the NVA was able to maintain a bombardment of about a thousand rounds per day into Khe-Sanh.

As I'm looking at the base, and wondering what it's like to take such a number of incoming, the pilot turns around and says, "Do you want to take pictures?"

"Of course."

"Sarge, open the hatch so she can lean out!"

He opens the hatch in the roof above me, and before I can think twice, I'm climbing on the jump seat armrest. I put my head out the hatch, using my elbows as tripods to brace myself, and start snapping pictures of the upcoming runway. This is certainly something I've never done before, and my anxious energy changes to excitement.

Now we're on the ground, rolling down the runway, and I'm getting carried away snapping pictures as we move by the base, until the pilot yells: "Thea, didn't you want to get out here?"

"Yeah."

"Well, you better go."

"You haven't stopped."

"We ain't gonna stop, baby. You better jump if you want to go. You better head out the back now."

I pull my gear together along with my Leica camera and run to the back of the cargo area. At the end of the long plane I see men push crates down the ramp, which keeps the base supplied. It's too dangerous to land here. As this thought comes to mind my apprehension returns because if this place is too dangerous for a plane to land, what about me?

I run off the ramp and onto the hard-packed dirt surface and look around as I slow down from running. I can feel their eyes on me from the mountains above. Just a moment ago I was looking down on them. Now I'm sure all eyes are on me—the only blond girl around for miles, and the only one alone in the middle of Khe-Sanh's runway. To add to my sense of comfort, the edge of the strip is littered with planes and helicopters that got hit and were pushed to the side and left there. The feeling I have is not a good one. Walking down the runway I hear the *click click* sound of incoming. Just a few yards off I see oil drums and throw myself behind them, hitting the ground hard as I land, bending my new lens cap in the process.

I realize this as I snap a picture of one of the strangest things I've seen before. In front of me, there are cows crossing the runway as they flee to save themselves. The fear in their eyes reminds me of something I saw in my childhood. After Soviet troops burned our Berlin apartment, my mother and I escaped the wrecked city to the country where my grandparents kept a cottage. Dead bodies were everywhere, but I remember crying when I saw a group of horses lying together in a ditch among rubble and blood. This was a cost of war rarely reported. You hear of the buildings smashed and burned and of the people dead and wounded, but rarely of the animals killed or the lovely tree, staple of your childhood backyard, shattered by mortars. These are terrible things also. They are part of the mood of war, and seeing the cows scatter with terror in their eyes brought me to the moment when we were also the victims of war.

It wasn't just the cows running from the plane that struck me but the oddity of cows on a military runway at all. I later learned the people in the village of Khe-Sanh, looking for safety, had brought their herds here. And so that's how you get cows on a runway dodging incoming.

But that didn't help my position now, behind oil drums. At the end of the airstrip, the C-130 banked over the trees for its return flight, followed by explosions on the runway. To my left Marines motion to me from the large green sandbag opening that leads to the base. The Marine closest to me is shouting: "Those drums are full of oil! Those drums are full of oil!"

I remember thinking: "Where else was a I supposed to go?" These were the only objects within a reasonable distance that I could have hid behind. Had one of the cows been hit, I suppose that might have served my purpose too. But the men here also just thought I looked funny. And they were right. A journalist scrambling for her life on an open runway was probably funny to some of the Marines under these conditions.

The incoming stops and somebody runs over from the sandbags and takes me inside. He grabs my arm and pulls me. I notice his hands are covered with red clay from where he grabbed me. I'm covered in the clay from diving on the edge of the strip. Everything is covered in it, even the oil drums have red smudges on their sides, and the green sandbag walls show the red streaks, especially down by the ground where the men kick it up. It's evening and it's just starting to get dark, but the red is clearly visible wherever you look.

As we enter the base, the man says: "You could have been killed."

"Well, how else was I supposed to get in?"

He doesn't respond. Who knows what he's thinking. Since it's dark now few Marines know there's a woman here, which may be better for now. The man I'm with takes me to the Marine Captain, whose job is to keep me alive and out of trouble. After a short introduction in the opening to a sandbag enclosure, the Captain walks me to the First Aid Tent. Inside is full of wounded men, mostly there from shrapnel. The ones who take direct fire don't make it here.

When I ask for the bathroom, he points it out to me just across from the First Aid Tent. I'm wearing fatigues and I have on a white Marine belt that was given to me by a friend. The trouble is that something is broken, and I can't get it off. It's dark and I can't see. I call the Captain, and he comes with a flashlight, and in the dark, holding possibly the only light in camp, he fumbles to undo my belt outside the latrine. I can only guess what the others think. There are a few laughs from somewhere indistinguishable as the Captain walks back to the tent alone. I follow shortly behind.

Without a word on the incident, the Captain puts me on a cot in a section of the Medical Tent where I'm mostly by myself. Soon the only thing I can think of is a shell dropping through the fabric above me. There's something about being attacked from above that's more unsettling than any other part of warfare. There's no action during the night, and so I sleep, but from time to time, and all night long, I hear the planes landing out on that strip. I can tell the deceleration and landing from the acceleration of the takeoff. The two come close together as the planes are not stopping throughout the night.

Next morning, I'm up early to tour the base. I want to see the ammo dump first—or what's left of it. The NVA really landed a blow when they hit that ammo dump, and it is important that I see the destruction. Word still hasn't spread that there's a woman in camp, but as I'm walking in the direction of the ammo dump I happen upon the open shower where the young Marines are bathing.

Here I am, a young blond German girl in the midst of a war, watching these young men shower. I'm a journalist, but when I see these young, fit men I pause without thinking. It's only a moment before they notice me standing there. The fact that I'm wearing fatigues apparently doesn't hide that I am a woman, and the men begin shouting, "Female in camp! Female in camp!" and boyishly run for their towels. I couldn't tell why they did that. I hadn't even taken pictures. Some of them blush, while others turn with towels on and stand, chests out, in more aggressive stances.

After the shower scene with the naked Marines, I continue on toward where the ammo dump was pointed out to me. It's not hard to find. Like the Captain said as he sent me in this direction, "You can't miss it." And you really can't. The ammo dump is now just one giant hole in the ground. When it blew up, it took nearly everything with it, and sent all types of munitions bouncing in every direction in camp and onto the runway itself. This is the reason the planes must land around the clock as they do, even risking coming down in broad daylight. If there's to be a full assault on the base, then they need every round they can get. With the explosion and subsequent damage, the Marines must get in more supplies so they don't run out of bullets when the shooting starts.

I talk out loud to my tape recorder and snap a few pictures. I notice a small dug-in bunker off to the side of the runway. I think this must be the tower where they direct landing planes, and since the base is under attack, the "tower" is underground and fortified. I make a note to get there after the briefing.

A few Marines are nearby as I look over the ammo dump. Suddenly I hear the *click click* sound, and the Marine closest to me shouts damn near in my ear, "Incoming!" I hit the red clay ground again, but I'm the only one. The other Marines stand there laughing as I dust myself off. The rounds were outgoing. I assume this is payback for witnessing some of them in the shower, but I can't be sure. A few of them look me over with less than friendly eyes.

We don't say another word to each other and I head off to the briefing. But since the briefing reveals nothing new, I walk out by the runway and enter the bunker. There are no flights scheduled to land for the next hour or so, so the man inside takes some time to talk with me. He's bored to tears.

This is not the assignment he planned on. "Sergeant Lan," he says to me, reaching out his hand. "Thea," I say. Despite the sunshine it's dark inside the bunker where he directs air traffic. Beneath a haze of smoke, he begins to talk. I guess since the Marines at Khe-Sanh were all in the same boat, and he had no one to talk to, he opened up to me. You might think the men were not fond of talking to journalists. I found it to be exactly the opposite.

Sergeant Lan is not where he wants to be, he tells me. Of course this goes without saying, since he's in Khe-Sanh, but in his case this is especially true. Until getting transferred here, Lan had it good in the Marines. He only arrived a few days before I did. Prior to this unfortunate deployment, he handled the Officers Bar and the Enlisted Men's Bar. He worked the supplies, but he also traded in money, wheeling and dealing in military payment certificates and cash. The PX wouldn't accept American dollars, only dealing in military scrip, and so he had what they called a "mamma sanh" in a nearby village who helped him exchange the money. He was running black market arbitrage and doing well. So well, in fact, that he had re-enlisted to keep his business. He had it in mind that he would supply the Americans in Japan. He probably read *Catch-22* and took that sort of military venture to heart. That was before he was sent here for a four-week stint in a fortified, underground airport tower, which saw constant assault.

At this point his dreams of building an empire in the Marine Corps were about as far away as possible.

"I won't leave this hole unless it's an urgent urgent." He says. "Just *urgent's* not enough to have me cross the open, not after the last few days."

"Today's not bad."

"Remember that when you cross back to the base," he said.

He's right. As I cross back in the open, I remember his words. Today isn't a bad day, but the silence is ruthless as I imagine the concussion that might come all of a sudden. I'm sure I'll hear the *click click* first, but God knows where it'll land.

Back in the base I see a French photographer. He's frantic because he just learned in a briefing that an offensive is on throughout the country. There is no cease-fire. It's obvious we have to get out. The action here at Khe-Sanh has died. We're in the wrong place. There's a war on after all, and it's my job to report from it.

CHAPTER 2

Nam O

Next morning we're on a helicopter out of Khe-Sanh. I arrived the 29th to stay through the 1st, but I got a ride out the 31st. Two full days without a shot fired is a long time, especially when the German Wire Service is pressing for twice daily news.

The flight from Khe-Sanh was uneventful, but I hit the ground running in DaNang and got over to the Press Center as fast as I could. First, I need to shower. This dust I'm covered in is awful and is giving my hair a red hue and texture I don't like. The Press Center's a good place to make connections and hear the news as well as clean up.

I quickly run to the showers and strip down, happy to have the hot water, but inside the shower stall I hear commotion outside. There's something happening. The journalists are getting excited, and if that's the case, then there's a story. I quickly get out of the shower and dress. With my boots in hand, I run out of the locker and see reporters assembling in Jeeps out in front of the center. I grab my recorder. In the street I jump into one of the Jeeps as they leave in a small convoy.

"Where we headed," I ask?

"Up the bay road, a place called Nam O."

And so it goes. I'm barefoot in the Jeep before I rub the dirt off my soles and put my boots on. My hair is still wet as we parallel DaNang Bay on the road up to the little village. It's such a lovely day, it's hard to imagine that people are fighting and dying—but they are. As the Tet offensive will show us, there is no front line in Vietnam. Fighting can take place anywhere, at any time. The driver and I say only a few words to each other, but enough so that I have a view on what's happening. There's word that Nam O has seen fighting in the last few hours, but the South Vietnamese, with some American advisors, pushed the NVA and Vietcong back and are now cleaning up.

As we arrive in Nam O the story we learn is different than what we heard. About five hundred meters from the village we run into a roadblock. The Vietcong, presumably, have cut trees across the main road of town every thirty yards or so, making travel by Jeep impossible. Not only that, but the South Vietnamese soldier who stops us is hesitant to let us in. It's unclear to him whether there's still fighting in the village. With a little persuasion, he lets us pass and we make our way to the village edge, which has been obscured by the crown of a large Hopea tree lying across the road. Passing that, we see a downed plane on the left side of the road. Inside, the pilot and co-pilot are dead behind the broken windshield. There's blood on their clothing. Beside the plane, South Vietnamese are using the first hut as a sort of makeshift headquarters. Out front, they have with them an NVA prisoner whose hands are bound.

I think to myself as I walk up to the hut, "This just happened." It's obvious to me that "cleaning up" didn't mean the mess after a battle, but rather a part of the battle itself. I walk toward the "headquarters." One of the South Vietnamese Airborne troops approaches me. He sees that I am wearing Airborne Wings on my chest and he points to them and smiles.

"What class you were?"

I tell him and ask what class he was in. We have an immediate connection because he knows I have gone through Airborne training, which I completed just a few weeks before the Tet offensive began. We can't stop and talk for long. He waves for me to follow him. We head up the road to the next house with a group of Airborne who are doing a sweep of the village. They've already taken a prisoner from a hut and are pulling him onto the street as I approach. He was holding a B-40 rocket, and the troops put that off to the side of the doorway.

The huts beside this one are all on fire. The Vietcong have lit the roofs. People are out in the streets shouting, but we are not prepared to put the village out. There's no way to do it. We can only stand and watch as it burns. I think of Morley Safer of CBS news covering the burning of Cam Ne by Marines, but these are NVA and Vietcong burning a South Vietnamese village. Because of the view of the war back in the United States, I imagine such an occurrence will hardly even matter—it's not the correct angle. If I were an American journalist, I probably wouldn't even do the story, but as a journalist for Germany I have more leeway.

Just then the troops I am following move up Main Street to the next house. As I walk with them I look across and see an NVA soldier with a B-40 rocket scurry behind one of the stone buildings for cover. Following close behind the NVA soldier is a South Vietnamese, but he doesn't know the other is present. I shout and wave to him. He just looks dumbfounded.

"There's an NVA with a B-40," I scream.

Before anyone on my side of the street can even comprehend what I've said, there's an explosion. It's not clear to me if this came from the NVA with the B-40 behind the stone building or somewhere else. As it turns out, there's a whole nest of NVA. What I know instead is the sense of hot air against my face. I hit the ground. The bullets are flying so close I hear the whiz before the crack of the rifle. I'm rolling toward the stump of a tree and reach for the black rubber tire I see lying out in the open. I try pulling the tire over my head, but it's too heavy, and I roll so the tire is between me and the fire. First oil drums, now a rubber tire for cover. I think I'm going to die. I don't mean that rhetorically.

I'm shouting into the microphone of my tape recorder: "There was an NVA with a B-40. Stone building." I am talking as if my words, my foreknowledge of the attack, can defend me against this moment. But as I heard a Marine say, "When the bullet's in the air, it's the king." I also had some notion that if I could only record what happened, it would be of some use, somewhere, to someone. But this is like chasing after the wind. I keep talking, "I can't die at 3:00 in the afternoon. It's sunny out." And now someone screams in English and breaks my own rant, "I'm hit! I'm hit!"

After the first intense seconds, where I count explosions and gunfire from many locations, I regain my composure. This tire won't stop an AK-47 round, and I keep rolling toward the stump. All of the troops I was with are also on the ground, until one of them jumps up to the stump of the tree. He opens fire, and gives us the cover we need to scamper behind him and the stump. This all takes place in under ten seconds, but it was like a day's worth of activity. I recall the pebbles in the street with granular detail.

Even with the Airborne returning fire, we are not safe. There are more explosions, and I hear an American advisor behind me calling in air support: "Danger close!" They are shouting. "Danger close!"

The voice says there's a whole company of Vietcong just ahead of us, using the stone building. The rest of the houses were wood huts that bullets simply whizzed through. The stone hut is the logical place to defend and attack.

Within moments bombs fall on the other side of the street and annihilate the stone building and all its inhabitants. More bombs fall, and the huts that were ablaze are blown into charred pieces. The fires are out, but there's no village left on that side of the street.

It's time for me to go, and I stand and head back toward where the Jeep is parked. On the way I learn the man who was screaming "I'm hit" is a cameraman. He's the lone casualty I hear of.

Back at the Press Center, I find a cot and turn in for the night. Nam O is the first close call I've had here. Up until this point death is just a thing that happens to other people. I don't know what I think of. It's not war. I get my mind as far from bullets and shooting as I can. On the morning of the 1st a chopper leaves for Hue where heavy fighting is reported and the Citadel is taken by the NVA.

I'm on that flight.

CHAPTER 3

Hue

I hit the ground running. Landing at Phu Bi just south of Hue turns out to be worse than landing at Khe-Sanh. At least there they had the good sense not to stop the plane. Here we're under direct mortar fire. It smells like war. I flew in with French photographers Francois Mazure and Cathy Leroy. We chatted on the flight over. It was pleasant, but it's a different story on the ground. Here, there's nowhere to hide and we run from the plane onto the open runway and jump into a huge concrete sewer pipe arranged at the side of the airfield.

This is a major American base that shouldn't be under attack like this. Something is wrong. The NVA and Vietcong are everywhere all at once. We run out of the pipes and toward the protection of the base. The noise doesn't stop. Planes are landing and taking off, while the mortars and artillery are exploding. Then the return shots come from the Americans trying to hone in on the Communists outside the city. There was a frantic atmosphere inside the base.

For some time now I've known about a group of German doctors who are stationed in the area. There are relatively few Germans in country and I typically know them all. This group was tending to anyone who came to them just outside of Hue: Vietcong, NVA, South Vietnamese, it didn't matter. But the doctors are in enemy territory now, since Tet began, and no one has heard from them.

I'll look for them if I can. I'm supposed to be going near where they were last seen, and the chopper there takes off in twenty minutes.

"Are you coming, Francois?"

But he and Cathy are talking. Maybe they think I don't speak French. I hear them, "Should we take her?"

"No, no. She is wearing a uniform. That will never do."

I don't care to ask. There's too much happening, and if they want to leave me, then okay. I'm supposed to be in Hue anyhow. They're headed there also, but instead decide to ride in on bicycles, which is insane. Of course they are captured. They are lucky to escape with their lives. Yet since the French are no longer enemies, the Communists treat them well and show them around. Their trip is good for propaganda. Of course Francois and Cathy must have known they were going to get taken; they weren't stupid. They must have planned for it. They brought back wonderful pictures. In fact, Cathy got a fantastic photo spread in Life Magazine out of it. But that's not for me. I have no intention of getting taken, nor of getting stuck anywhere, including Hue. I get onto the chopper determined to get back out again so I can file my stories in the next 24 hours.

As it turns out, the city of Hue is overrun with NVA and VC. The Marines and some Army are fighting house-to-house. We land at an old hotel, which is now the Military Assistant Command, Vietnam (MACV) compound. It's near the river. The walls are huge, ten or twelve feet, and before we land within their safety I see down into the mess of streets below. Many of the buildings have roof terraces, which are a haunt for snipers, making it rather difficult for the Americans to move around in the city. Then the wall draws up in front of me and I'm out of the chopper into the MACV compound now serving as the American base.

The whole city is lost. The Americans have just this piece of land in the extreme south up against the Perfume River. They've even lost the Citadel, the old Imperial Palace full of anthropological treasures, across the river. There's nothing that can be done there now, as the Americans have orders not to heavily bombard the Palace. This would be like bombing the Smithsonian in D.C. or the Forbidden City in Beijing. And the Americans want to avoid doing that.

It's chaotic on the ground. Marines are leaving to head into town. They don't know it, but they are headed in the direction the five

German doctors were last seen. I immediately get into the group and ask if we can look for the doctors.

"All right," a Marine sitting atop a tank shouts to me. "Stick close behind."

The street is small and old; it's surrounded by three and four-story masonry buildings, some with courtyards, others not. There are one or two burned-out cars and piles of rubble where building facades were blasted off. Immediately we begin taking fire. There's a sniper on the next block. The Marines in the open take cover with us behind the tank. "Don't even put your head out there," one says. "It's accurate fire."

They call on the radio for some close air support to see if they can kill the sniper. There's no waiting. The green chopper comes fast over the compound wall right over our heads. The noise is startling.

The chopper hovers over the road, the river to its right, running perpendicular with the street, and the gunner opens fire on the small grove from inside the chopper. They used to drop defoliants on the jungle to burn off cover. The bullets from this helicopter have a similar effect on the foliage of this small grove. If anyone was there, he is now dead. The helicopter then elevates and opens fire into one of the rooftop terraces. It's hard to tell from where I stand if he actually got the sniper or not. In a moment or two we begin moving up the road again and immediately come under fire and the Marines pull back. We won't advance up this street.

That's it. We can't very well take casualties or deaths when they are avoidable. The doctors won't be found today. I'm sorry about that, but there's really very little I can do.

Back inside the compound I meet the wife of the university director, which is very near to the hotel where the Americans have established their base. She also has the five German doctors on her mind. Their heroism and determination to help people in this war has made a great impression on her. We talk about the doctors and rationalize their well-being. Of course because the doctors were doing good for people without discrimination, they will be left alone. At least the moral code we assume is universal dictates that they would be spared. And though I feel somewhat comforted by our talk, I am not at all convinced. I just hope they are all right. With any luck the Americans will retake the city and surrounding area in the coming days and the doctors will be safe.

To that effect, South Vietnamese Airborne troops have already marched in to retake the Citadel on the other side of the Perfume. The fighting is heavy over there. We hear the constant echo of gunfire and explosions, and it's tempting to make the trip. I decide against it after all. But there's a crew from ABC, which arrived the same day as I did in Hue. They go to the Citadel and actually get inside. This would make for a great story, except they get trapped there for a week. When I see the Japanese photographer from the group after the event, he says to me, "I will follow Miss Thea. Wherever she goes, there is action."

"Then you should follow me out too," I say. He laughs.

That's when I learn of what the fighting was like on the other side of the river. I make my way to the South Vietnamese Airborne Base in Saigon, where I meet with captain Le Vanh Manh who marched in to retake the Citadel. He tells me their story.

The Citadel of Hue is an old fort, built with meter thick walls, surrounded by moat-like ditches. The old Emperors Palace lay inside with gardens and ponds, housing most of Vietnam's historic treasures. It stands on the north side of the river across from the new section of Hue. There are also two bridges, car and railroad, crossing the Perfume that connect both sides of the city.

After the Tet Offensive caught the troops around the Citadel unprepared, the 2nd and 7th battalion of the Vietnamese Airborne march into Hue. The soldiers aren't used to long marches and discard much of their provisions on the way. This is a mistake, of course. It takes days for them to get inside. Even American Marines are repelled from taking the Citadel via the road bridge. And for the South Vietnamese Airborne, the fighting is house-to-house.

Captain Le Vanh Manh tells me they are terribly hungry because they discarded so much of their food on the march in. And there's something else that is disturbing for the troops. The Vietcong know the South Vietnamese by name. In Captain Manh's case, the Vietcong call out to him: "Hey, Captain Manh, we know all about your family in Saigon." They are shouting this over a bullhorn as he calls in orders on the radio. For a moment he stops to hear them. It's not often the enemy knows you personally by name, and he wonders how this is so. "You think your family is safe, but you are lying to yourself."

Manh assumes they must know his name because of papers he dropped on the long march in. He is disheartened but continues to fight. It's not until the 6th of February that his battalion is relieved. The fighting is so personal; the trapped ABC team relays as much to me. But it's not something I'll see. When the ABC team leaves for the Citadel, I decide it's time to go back to DaNang. I want to file my story, and I know that doing so will mean having to go to Saigon, which will be difficult. DaNang is the first step.

Down by the river I see two men preparing a small plane for takeoff. From where I stand it looks like they are filling the back of the two-seater with document boxes. It's not long before I reach them on foot. The university was only fifty yards or so from the river.

"Hey, can I catch a ride with you guys outta here?"

"I think we'll be too heavy. Besides, we don't have another seat."

"I don't need a seat. I can squeeze in behind you."

They look at each other. I think that if I were a male they would say no. Instead they tell me to come on. But he really isn't lying about the weight problem.

"It's not that we're too heavy to fly. It's that we're too heavy to take off from this short runway."

I am stuffed partially between and behind the two seats that make up the cockpit of this small plane. From where I sit, I have a fine view out the windshield. I realize then what I should have realized a moment ago: this is not a runway at all. It's a flood plain beside the river where maybe a few trees have been taken out to accommodate chopper landings. At the end of what we are calling a runway is a cluster of trees and a few houses. In other words, my additional weight, however slight, might be the straw that broke the camel's back.

As we accelerate down the runway, the pilot shouts, "Pray that we clear those trees." We do as he says, and the plane heads directly for the trees. We are lifting up, but painfully slowly. I think that we won't make it after all. The pilot should have known better than to stuff this silly plane full of stacks of paper and then try and take off on a short runway.

"We've got it," the copilot says, and we all begin shouting as we clear the trees and are off into the sky. Not only have we survived this shoddy runway and an overstuffed plane, but we also escaped from the open battle of Hue, which is a great feeling. It's like being freed, and while it's possible we might get shot down from the sky, I'm not thinking about that right now.

CHAPTER 4

Saigon

DaNang is a fairly secure city. There have been some VC incursions nearby, but for the most part we are insulated from the Tet Offensive.

On the ground at the airport, I say goodbye to my fellow travelers. They want to have a drink.

"I'm sorry, but I can't. I have to see if I can get back to Saigon to file my stories."

"Good luck with that, honey, but Saigon's a no-go for a while."

I know as well as he does what's happening. In Khe-Sanh when we first got word that Tet began, we also learned that Saigon was seeing heavy fighting. In fact, the main attack has taken place at Tan Son Nhat Airport, where I would have to land. It's gotten so bad that there's fear the international airport and the base itself may be entirely overrun. This means that flying all the way down there is damn near impossible, but that doesn't mean we can't land under fire. After all, I've done it before. It's also not possible that all the flights have ceased. Someone still has to fly in. The Americans still have air superiority. With a little luck and some work, I know I can get back with my stories in reasonable time, despite what that pilot says.

At the Press Center I run into a pack of journalists all with the same problem. We had been in dangerous locations and were looking to get our stories out. The only way for anyone to do that is to get to Saigon. We all know it. At first there's almost a competition. It happens quietly as people tap their sources to see if there's any way out. But, as it becomes apparent that no one has a flight, we all begin to brainstorm together. Only after deciding we can't do it individually do we decide to do it collectively. I believe it was a journalist at *Time Magazine* who mentioned the possibility of a tactical flight leaving for Saigon. Tac flights deliver important papers back and forth from various locations in country. The flights are based out of Tan Son Nhat. It's only natural that we try to get on. We find the plane at the airport, and all approach as a group. The pilot is nonplussed by this gaggle of reporters with hands out. It's obvious we can't all fit.

"I can take one of you." The pilot says. There is a sort of mumbling that consumes us for a moment. Then we fix the problem quickly by drawing straws. Journalists may be a competitive bunch, and ambition in wartime can often cause serious repercussions, but when it comes down to it, we all help each other.

I pull the shortest straw, which in this case means I win. Now everyone begins handing me their stories, or their film in bags marked for their network. This is no light task.

The flight over to Tan Son Nhat is uneventful. We land without difficulty, but on the runway a Lieutenant Colonel, the Public Affairs Officer (PAO), meets me at the ladder. He's nervous. It' obvious why, since there are mortar rounds landing within a hundred yards of where we stand. We quickly run over to the Jeep and speed away to his office. Why should this airport be any different from the others where I've been the last few days? But this *is* different. This is Saigon. The capital of the South. How on earth did the Communists get here in such strength to actually threaten the airport? It doesn't matter at this point. What matters is that I'm here at Tan Son Nhat, and I still can't get back to Saigon. There is a curfew, and the Vietcong are scattered here and there between the airport and downtown. I'll have to stay inside the Public Affairs Office tonight. We're apparently safe here, so they say, but I at least have to try to get out. I get a phone call through to my husband Dick Rosenbaum at the Caravelle Hotel. He's ABC's Bureau Chief.

"They'll shoot you to pieces," he says.

I press him because I need to get in to file my stories, but there's nothing he can do tonight with a curfew and the VC.

In the morning he calls back to the PAO. He's organized a chopper to get me and the others here back to downtown Saigon. The chopper will pick us up in front of the PAO and drop us off on the roof of the American Embassy.

We wait for the chopper to arrive. When it does, we quickly run out and get on board. There are still mortars falling on the runway. How accurate they are is hard to tell, though you don't want to wait to find out. It's just a quick jump over to downtown from the airport. But as with anything else, it's always something simple that can get you killed. There are plenty of reporters and military personnel who only had a quick flight to take that ended their lives. Once you're in the sky, you're at the mercy of a lot of things far outside your control. A bullet fired from the ground is just one of those.

However, in this case we fly up to the American Embassy without trouble. From above, the city has much the same appearance as Hue did. You can tell there's been heavy fighting in some spots. Smoke is still coming out from a few buildings, but it looks as if the worst has passed.

The helicopter touches down, and I smile when I see my husband standing in the stairwell opening on the roof. He is happy to see me, but then he's shouting and waving his hands. It doesn't register to me why. I walk off the helicopter toward where he stands beneath the spinning rotors. There is tremendous noise.

He yells in my ear: "You were taking sniper fire."

"I didn't know. I couldn't hear."

Other Bureau Chiefs are there with him waiting for the precious story bags I've brought along. These bags represent so much. Several reporters were nearly killed covering their stories; now all their efforts live inside a simple bag.

It's then that I see down into the courtyard, where there is a hole in the outer wall facing the street and bullet marks everywhere. The American Seal and flag are laying on the ground. The Seal itself has bullet holes in it. Vietcong actually got inside the compound of the American Embassy. The fighting was hand-to-hand before the intruders were killed. The attack by the Vietcong was worse here than I would have imagined possible before Tet began. I certainly wasn't the only one who viewed American strength relative to NVA and Vietcong weakness in this way. Now there was some question about how strong the Americans really were.

As it turns out, the event helps reduce the American public's appetite for war. I begin by filing a story of the moment in Saigon, and then working my way backwards from there.

It's right in the midst of this, maybe a few days after my return from DaNang, that I begin to have pain. I see that I am bleeding. Dick and I are in our hotel room. It's night and I'm frightened. Dick tries comforting me, but he doesn't know what's wrong. Then I tell him. After a few hours we have an idea of what's wrong. We had not known that I was pregnant, but it seems likely that I miscarried.

Dick seems certain of it. In the morning, a doctor confirms our suspicion. This is a blow to me, but I try not to linger in the sadness of the idea of losing a child. Saigon is under attack, actively so, and it's easy to lose myself in the swirl of the war, which is now coming apart before the Americans' eyes. The significance of the Tet Offensive on the American psyche probably can't be overestimated. The war is already unpopular; now it's a quagmire.

As part of this quagmire, I hear of fighting out near Cholon, which is the so-called "Chinatown" of Saigon. Dick and I began frequenting this part of town when Dick found a restaurant serving wonderful winter kimchi, a tasty Korean specialty. But the days of having a nice dinner in Cholon are now over. We often took people from out of town there. Now it's the center of heavy fighting and massive fires. The district consists mostly of tightly packed wooden structures. It happens now that the VC set fires as a diversion to escape. As is typical of this moment, the fighting is house-to-house.

There is no battle line. Now this is true generally of the fighting in Vietnam, but during Tet, and in Saigon, if you went to an area where fighting was underway, you'd have great difficulty in pointing to one side of the street or the other and saying with any certainty, "That is where the Vietcong are and that is where the South Vietnamese are." You just couldn't do it with any consistency.

I get into this neighborhood near Cholon by driving from the hospital where I had been volunteering. As it is, I am supposed to be taking it easy. I am still feeling sick, but staying still makes me more miserable. And so I go into the city. I drive my own car out to Cholon, park, and follow some South Vietnamese soldiers into a group of buildings. As we get inside, one of the soldiers points to the ceiling above our heads and tells us to be quiet.

"Shhh." He says with his finger before his mouth. Then we hear noises above us. The Vietcong are on the roofs. This is not good. I have to get out of here. We move to the next house and hear them above us as well. They are chasing us from house to house. And so we get out into the streets and all of a sudden the block goes up in flames. They just want a way out, I think. The VC are afraid of the Americans and South Vietnamese who are coming in force now.

I am standing on the corner with a car in front of me, trying to make a decision about which way I should run, or which way is safe to keep my back to. That's when a man walks up on his bicycle. He throws it down on the ground, kneels before me and starts begging with his hands folded and pointing up toward me, "Please help me. Save me. Save me."

I am just a young girl. This is an old man. How inhumane can war be? This poor man, who has so much tradition, is throwing himself onto the ground in front of a white, young woman to beg for his life. I don't know what to do. I pick him up with his bike and help guide him out of the fire zone there. But my heart is absolutely beating. These people must hate us. They are so full of horror and fear. I had been through it as a small child in World War II. This is what we went through. I remember it in Berlin. It's the poor civilians who get hurt, or the poor, low-level G.I.s who get killed.

CHAPTER 5

Berlin

Civilians take the brunt of war.

My mom and I were living in an apartment while my dad was away fighting on the Eastern Front. The city of Berlin only recently came under bombardment from the Allies. Other cities had been hit. Until today, Berlin had been spared.

My father told us repeatedly that when the bombing starts, take refuge in the shelters across the street at the Botanical Gardens. Now the bombing begins. I don't know what's happening as it starts. I remember my mother taking me by the hand and leading me across the road. Another man from our apartment building comes alongside me and takes my other hand. We reach the Gardens. The grounds are expansive. There is a full moon. It's very bright. There is a couple ahead of us on the path inside the gardens, and they are pointing to the sky. The moon there is large over the horizon, and I see what they are pointing at. Without a sound, bombs fall in little rows in front of the white backdrop. It is as beautiful as it is awful.

We run to the nearest shelter. But this one is not finished and is already overcrowded. The people inside tell us we cannot stay. We run out into the open and find refuge in another shelter. That night the bombs do not fall on our part of Berlin. We are lucky in this way. But my mother resolves never to leave our own apartment building to find shelter in the Gardens again.

In the basement of our large building there are shelters set up with field beds and other necessities. Many people have taken refuge here. This place will be as safe as the Gardens when the bombs fall. There's no need to run out in the open and expose ourselves to more danger. Especially when we learn that Volker has died of scarlet fever in the garden shelter across the street. His parents were best friends with mine, and his sister Elke was exactly my age. We played together, and I remember when her little brother was born in their apartment. I wasn't there when he died. My friend Elke tells me about it. "He is dead," she says. But I don't know what that means. She says she was there, and he was in his crib and opened his eyes and looked at them, and then he closed his eyes and never opened them again. I don't think she knows what it means either. But she knows he is not here anymore.

From that point on, the bombing gets worse, but the bombs are not so terrible as our fear of the Russians. They are closing in on the city. Can the Wehrmacht, the German armed forces, really allow that? The answer will not come for weeks, but in that time we must sustain the bombings. And then they come. These men have engaged in the most brutal fighting in history, and now they are here. And they have been given three days of carte blanche. Rape and murder commence as soon as they breach the city. Women are raped not once or twice, but repeatedly. It is a curse to be beautiful. It is a curse to be alive. And my mother is very beautiful.

One morning the Soviet troops enter our basement. They select one woman from our group to rape. For whatever reason they do not choose my mother. Then for the next two days they return at various times looking to take the poor woman out again. They return a final time. They do not seem to care which woman goes with them. The other people in the basement plead with the first victim to go. She has already been five times or so, but they beg her to go nevertheless. They say that if she doesn't, then someone else will have to go, and since she has already done it, then it wouldn't be that bad for her again; for a new woman, however, it would terrible.

She goes with them.

The Soviets are living in our building while we hide in the basement. They know we are there, of course. Many of these Soviet conscripts think the toilets are used for washing potatoes. On more than one occasion, angry Soviet soldiers come barging into our basement, demanding to have their potatoes back. They have flushed them down the toilet and are angry at the faulty German engineering, which loses the potatoes it's supposed to wash. This would be funny, however, the soldiers are not at all amused. They really want their potatoes back. My mother says they must all be farm boys who have never seen indoor plumbing.

One morning two Soviet soldiers enter our bunker again. I do not recall the smell of booze, however, that was certainly prevalent among the victors. It is just my mother and me in the little room. They rummage our things. My mother stands with me beside her. One of the soldiers touches my hair and places me on his lap. "Do you know Hitler, little girl?"

"Who is he?" I say. "A neighbor?" I am only four years old.

He smiles. But they do nothing further, and leave as quietly as they came. In hindsight these two were not out of control. Maybe they had been recently satiated and so they left us alone. But they frighten my mother. There have been other children taken and shipped to Siberia simply for the cruelty of the act. This is not victory; this is revenge—to break the pride of the Germans. And when my mother learns the two soldiers are back in the building, she hides me. She lifts up the blankets we have on the upper bunk of the field bed and lays me down. Putting the blankets over me, she says: "Don't breathe. Don't say anything. Don't do anything."

The same two soldiers return. "Where is she?"

"She's no longer here," mother says. The men tell her that it will be her turn next if she doesn't give me up. Again she tells them that I am gone. They search the whole cellar but can't find me. For some reason they leave. But they want to retaliate. The soldiers have been misinformed and believe our building is Nazi housing. It's not, that building is a block away, but this doesn't stop them from torching our apartment building. They don't care that they've made a mistake. They are here expressly to cause terror.

We have to go. I leave my doll Peter behind but I want to return and get him. My mother won't let me. We head into the courtyard. There is a woman there, lying on her stomach. I recognize her. She is a neighbor. "Mommy, why is Mrs. Schumann lying on her stomach?"

"She's dead."

That word again: "What's death?"

"Let's go. We have to leave."

They are shooting at us as we go. The building is burning, and there is artillery fire all around. I have a little nap sack, and I cling to it as we start running down the street with many other people.

There is an address that I have been made to learn since the war began. It's the address of my grandmother's house outside the city. However, getting there is difficult. The city is overrun by troops who are absolutely out of control. It is as if they are on holiday. We are pushing a carriage along with us as we walk out of the city. At times my mother lets me ride in it, but for the most part we have our packs stored in there and so I must walk. That's when a military vehicle driven by drunken soldiers drives up over the curb. The city is their apocalyptic playground. They don't come toward us with any maliciousness. They are unconscious we are there. Instead, they must be joy riding.

Mother and I run from the oncoming truck, but there is a large fence alongside the road, and we have nowhere to run to. I remember climbing up the fence with my mother and clinging there like frightened insects. From this position we might be safe from the oncoming truck. They never reach us though. Instead their dirty green lorry smashes into some trees that stand near the roadside. If the men inside are hurt, we don't wait to find out. My mother takes me by the hand, and we continue walking. Wherever we can, we take to back roads, or walk through backyards. At night we stay in the famed Schreber Gardens. These are small allotments of land in the city where people used to grow vegetables and fruit. Inside, the people are not supposed to have any permanent structures, but the Germans overdo everything, and so many of these gardens are very nice indeed. Some have bathrooms and kitchens and other permanent facilities. They serve us well as we make our trek out of Berlin. The Gardens are also surprisingly devoid of rampaging soldiers.

It is several days before we make it out of the city and to my grandmother's. How long it takes us I don't know exactly. I only know that it seems to me a long time. We are always hiding. We have very little food, and my mother is always worried that we will run into the Soviets, who we now know can and will do anything they want to us.

Then I suddenly begin to recognize where I am. I recognize the streets, the trees, the neighborhood. It's grandmother's house. More rightly, this is grandmother's summer house. It's a small cottage outside Berlin in a country setting that made an excellent place to escape to in the summer. It makes an equally good place to escape in war. My whole family has been told to run here in case of an emergency if they can. All of my young relatives, myself included, have memorized the address and general location of the small town of Kleinmachnow on a map so that we can find it if we ever wind up near the area.

This precaution has served us very well indeed. However, the house has not held up through the war as we would have liked. Only parts of the kitchen and a few other sections remain. The rest has been blown away by an errant bomb. As my family's home was not a target and nothing else in the area had been bombed, we all assume that this was some kind of accident. The pilot couldn't return to his base in the U.K. after bombing Berlin without dropping his full load. For whatever reason, one of the bombs sticks, and he ends up releasing it "harmlessly" over the countryside and it blows the back off our refuge, nearly killing my grandmother. This is the way of war. One man's mistake is another man's horror.

Many years later, I took the only flight back to Saigon from visiting the Montagnards. These people were indigenous to Vietnam and lived in the mountains. They hated the Vietnamese and were friendly to the Americans. It goes without saying, but they hardly exist anymore. My flight back was on a small bomber, an A34, and the pilot was on a run. He dove several times and delivered his payload. But it turned out that one of the bombs did not fall and was still attached to the wing. We couldn't land with it there. We eventually got it to drop. But as with the bomb that struck my grandmother's house, this bomb just fell into the countryside wherever we could get rid of it. Only God knows if it struck some poor villager's hut or killed his cattle.

My grandmother, Omi in Prussian German, was in the kitchen at the time when the bomb hits. She could have been killed. Instead, it just took off the back of the house and left a crater in the yard. But this complicates things because we can't stay there with her and my grandfather, whom we call Opi, as we had hoped. There just isn't enough room with Omi and Opi since much of the house is either missing or open to the outdoors.

Opi doesn't want us to stay anyhow. My mother is very beautiful and that's one of the most dangerous things a woman can be right now. Shortly after our arrival, he sends us away to the neighbors' house which wasn't bombed. They've abandoned their home so we have it all to ourselves. There we stay in the basement, which is fine for a few days, but then the Soviets arrive.

We're quiet in the basement when two Soviet soldiers walk through the door. I have seen soldiers and am not immediately frightened by them. My mother is though. By looking at them, she must know what they have come for. She grabs me and tells me not to let her go. She is lying on the bed with me on her stomach and we are clinging to each other. One of the soldiers sits at the foot of the bed and tries coaxing me to him, "Come here, little girl. It will be all right if you just come here." The other soldier rolls on top of me. He is trying his best to tear me from my mother. But we are clinging to each other with every ounce of strength. She is saying, "Don't let go." And I am frantic. I'm screaming like a crazy person and kicking my feet, while the man at the end of the bed is like a Siren to me. I want to go to him badly. I just want this to stop. But my mother is saying, "Don't let go," and I am screaming.

This continues long enough that the soldier who has been trying to get me and my mother apart gets angry. He then slashes us with his bayonet. But we have several layers of clothing on and the wounds we suffer are superficial. The two then leave the basement. Why should they go through so much trouble just to rape a woman? They move along.

CHAPTER 6

Berlin

"Will they return?" This is the question my mother asks herself. We wonder if there's some way that my grandfather could have protected us. But the soldiers would have gladly used him for target practice. Later I think maybe this would have been better.

However, my grandmother did not stand for any bad behavior from these soldiers. There was a time when the soldiers arrived, looking for watches. They used to go about saying, "Uri, Uri, Uri." This meant "watch."

My grandfather fixed watches, and some of the neighbors must have confessed this to the soldiers. The soldiers soon arrived looking for his cache. They were enamored with watches, which, considering many had never seen indoor plumbing, was not out of character. They were also very young, and when they approached my grandmother's house and entered to pillage, my grandmother slapped the first one across the face.

"Nix, Uri," she said.

The man was ashamed and backed out of the house, apologizing and calling her "Mother." "Sorry, Mother," he said. "Sorry, Mother." She was a formidable woman.

During our stay there, she told us that my cousins arrived weeks earlier. They had since moved on, but what they endured is worth noting. They feared the Soviets and were doing their best to stay ahead of them, hopefully even making it to the West, and to the Americans.

We, however, had not had that plan, and had already met our Soviet conquerors.

My cousins lived in East Prussia. Their town, Preussisch Holland (Prussian Holland), was on low-lying land near the Baltic. Centuries ago, engineers from Holland came to build flood control, hence the name. The so-called Polish Corridor separated East Prussia from Germany then. Despite the distance, the people there were extremely German and independent. They were also, unfortunately, among the first to begin screaming "Heil Hitler." And it was in East Prussia, in a section now Poland, where Hitler installed his Wolf's Lair, a series of heavily fortified bunkers that housed much of his government. Until '44, East Prussia saw very little war.

My young cousin, Helmut, was sixteen at the time and the eldest of three: Hanna the youngest, his sister, and Klaus. Helmut had to go into the Hitler Youth. But he liked it because he had the chance to play sports and to socialize with boys his age. He also learned woodworking, which became a lifetime passion. But East Prussia was not long for the world. The Russians were fast pushing westward. Hitler knew this. He fled, and had the Wolf's Lair demolished. But he would not allow the German people left behind to flee. The Gestapo said any German caught running would be shot. The Gestapo was the Nazi's secret police force and was more than capable of enforcing the edict.

Then suddenly in Prussian Holland, there was an influx of wounded German soldiers. They transformed the school into a field hospital. Helmut's little sister helped out, knitting socks for the soldiers. But the army was retreating, and fast. At night Helmut saw fires on the horizon. The Soviets were just outside the town. He could hear the gunfire, artillery, and the screech of Katyusha rockets mounted on American-made Studebakers. He knew it was time to go.

Helmut's aunt came to the same conclusion. Her sister, Helmut's mother, was in the hospital and was not ready to leave. Helmut and Auntie Max picked up Helmut's mother from the hospital, holding her up and urging her on. "We have to leave," they told her. Helmut's father was gone in the war. His aunt was a schoolteacher, and she resolved that whatever happened, she would get the rest of her family out of East Prussia. The window to escape was narrowing. They either had to go right then, or stay for the Soviets. They chose to leave. There were few ways out. Several extended members of the family attempted to flee over a bay to the icy Baltic, where they were bombed.

Helmut and his aunt took a different route. While the roads were clogged with soldiers, trains still left daily. The five—Helmut, his mother, his aunt, young sister, and brother—went to the town train station, where they heard of a train leaving for Berlin. The train did not leave that day and they had to return home. Finally, on January 21ˢᵗ, 1945, they finagled their way onto the last train out of East Prussia. The train was a work train for the railroad company. They shared a boxcar with German soldiers and other refuges. The train was full of German soldiers. At this point, Nazi officials and the Gestapo did not inhibit the evacuation of East Prussia. However, since they waited to the last moment, the flight of Germans was a mess. Many died.

Inside the car there was only room for his mother, aunt, and two siblings. As Helmut was the man of the family now, he sat out in the open in a pile of coal. It was just him and another man, freezing. The temperature was negative 41 degrees Fahrenheit—extremely cold. It was the coldest winter on record. Outside the train, people were frozen in the roads; people were openly murdered by the Red Army. If they took boats, they were sunk in the Baltic by the Russian Navy.

The train stopped at the Weichsel River on top of a bridge. The soldiers laid mines. Helmut watched them. It took almost all night, and it was so cold. Then the soldiers jumped back onto the train, and the bridge detonated as they pulled away. This truly was the last train from East Prussia. As they passed, so too did the world they knew for so long. The Germans were doing everything in their power to slow the advance of the Soviets. At least on the train there was a sense the Soviets could not get them. But what was happening behind them was terrible. Those who couldn't escape were at the mercy of the Red Army. Shortly after the war, just about every German was expelled from East Prussia. The country was split in half; the southern half was Polish and the northern was Russian. This was hard on those whose families had lived there for generations. Many simply could not survive as refugees.

I had another aunt and uncle in the region. They were real Nazis. He was the director of a school. He knew the Russians were coming but believed to the end that Hitler was going to save him. Of course Hitler wasn't going to save anyone, and so this aunt and uncle hung themselves from the oven doors before the Russians could get them. The Russians shot another cousin because they assumed he was old enough to be a soldier, and since he was not fighting, he must be a deserter.

But Helmut was lucky in this way. They escaped just ahead of the advancing Soviets in East Prussia. They stayed two weeks with my grandmother; this was sometime before my mother and I arrived. Then they decided the Russians were coming there too, and they had to go. They went to Berlin and got onto a train headed farther west into Germany. They wound up in the town of Bremen near the North Sea. After some time in American and British refugee and P.O.W. camps, they were released. They faced hardship, but nothing like they would have seen had they remained in East Prussia or lingered at my grandmother's house

My grandmother was also East Prussian German, but she and her sister had moved to the capital of Berlin of their own free will many years before. They were adventurous. Grandmother was pregnant five times, but only two of the children survived childbirth; one was my father. She was the family's rock. We returned to her time and time again.

My memory of these days, while clear, is difficult for me to understand.

After my mother was attacked, she decided we were not safe there. She may have suspected that her father-in-law had informed on her. We headed back to Berlin. She had word that a friend there had an open apartment for us, so we left on foot. The Gardens were still where we stayed most nights. There were refugees everywhere. Since the Allies turned much of the city to rubble, there was no place to live. We still saw Russian soldiers, but the dogs were off. The commanding officers must have reigned in their subordinates. We no longer saw the roving drunken soldiers as we had seen in the immediate aftermath of invasion. The closer to the city center we got, the worse grew the destruction.

In Berlin, we waited in lines for food and water with the other refugees. Many had been victimized in the cruelest ways. Other simply lay dead among the rubble.

Soon the Allies came and divided the city. We were in the Allied Sector of Berlin and acquired a small apartment. There our relatives came and went. Berlin is where the Cold War began, but they had not yet built the Berlin Wall, and we could move about rather freely. We were not constantly harassed for our papers as in later times. We even traveled to the eastern sector of Berlin to buy food because it was cheaper there with the Russians.

We went to my grandmother's house frequently. Now we didn't have to hide on our way. We went there for visits and to get away from the city for the weekend. I was standing in the kitchen of their house some months after the war. Opi, my grandfather, must have made some makeshift enclosure, which by that point was to close the house off. That's when a German soldier walked into the backyard.

It was my father.

CHAPTER 7

Post War

Omi is first to recognize him. She shouts. My mother follows suit and so do I when I see my dad. We all run up and hug him in his uniform.

Before his arrival, it was impossible to know where he was. There were so many men who never came back from the war. They just went away to the East, and that was that. You never talked about it. We had no way of knowing if he was alive. He had been in a British P.O.W. camp. They would have released him, but he needed to be de-Nazified. That's what the Allies called it. The Soviets called it re-education, or Siberia.

Mom married Dad during the war. My mother was very beautiful, almost exotic. She had black hair, with brown skin and extremely blue eyes. My father was just dashing, tall, slim, and good-looking. He came home on leave for the wedding. She borrowed a dress. That was 1939. I was born a year later. Now it was '45, and my mother had hardly seen him, except on those occasions when he was on leave. Imagine going on leave during such a war and then having to go back? Or getting married to a soldier who went from the altar back to the front?

But now he was home and things could become normal. As normal as can be expected. At this point, the back of the house was still missing. My grandfather was working to repair it. Even after my father returned, we continued making the weekend trips out to

Kleinmachnow to see my grandparents. My parents must have thought it was nice to leave the havoc of the city. I liked to be out in the country. I also liked it when my grandfather told me stories of his time in Africa. He would take me on his lap and remember when he was a soldier and spent time with the Pygmies. I loved to hear those stories of the German colonies. The world he described was so far away, it seemed it couldn't be real.

That's when a strange thing happened. My father came home with a package of cheese. I remember being excited by the cheese. It was hard to get hold of any food and just this little bit, just a small block, was a luxury to us. My father was proud.

I don't remember where he put the cheese, but when we returned later to enjoy it with our dinner, it was missing. I was as surprised by this as anyone. My father was angry. He turned to his father: "Did you eat the cheese?"

"No."

He went around the room like this, until he came to me. We were standing in the kitchen by the dark wood table. They were all looking down to me, but I hadn't stolen the cheese, so I felt as innocent as a bird.

"Thea," my father said.

"Yes, Daddy."

"Did you eat the cheese?"

"No, Daddy. I didn't eat the cheese."

Now the whole family is looking at me as if I stole it, as if I am a liar. But I'm not a liar. I know that. However, all these adults know differently—their very stern faces tell me so. Each of the adults was looking forward to having a bite of that cheese as much as I was.

"Thea. We know you ate the cheese. Please just admit it."

"But, Dad, I didn't eat the cheese."

"Tell the truth. No one else ate the cheese. You had to have eaten the cheese. I won't hurt you. You won't be punished if you just tell me the truth. But I won't have you lying to me, either."

I was terribly conflicted. They were all looking at me as if I was bad. I didn't even know where he put the cheese. I was looking forward to having it myself. But they all seemed to believe that I had done it. If I told him a lie, he would believe it as the truth, but the truth was a lie and brought punishment.

"Yes, Daddy. I ate the cheese."

My father was true to his word, and I was not punished. I was only five years old. I didn't dwell too much on this apparent contradiction, but I didn't forget it, either. The end of the weekend came and we rode the train back to Berlin.

Food was extremely short then. There were bread lines. And we had ration cards, which allowed us to get a certain amount of food. With that, you could go to the baker and get maybe half a loaf of white bread, and maybe half a loaf of black bread. You were also given an amount of grease because there wasn't any butter, as well as some flour.

We happened to live across from the baker, but this didn't make getting food easier. The lines were always long there. And even if you got through the line, you weren't guaranteed that they would have food.

I was always in the streets then, so I knew my way around our part of the city. I knew not to go with strangers; my parents had told me that. I especially knew the bakery because so many people came there. It smelled so good that it was a draw. And then one night, my mother looked out the window. She saw that the line was short. "Thea, would you go down and see if you can get some bread?" She gave me the rations card and told me to bring back half a loaf of white bread and one loaf of black bread. "You can remember all that, right?"

"Yes, half a loaf of white bread and one loaf of black bread."

I was so proud. This was the first job I had been given. I ran out the apartment door, down the stairs and out to the street below. It was sunny. I'm sure my mother watched as I crossed. I didn't look to see though. I got into line and waited there like the adults were doing. When it was my turn, I walked up to the counter, proud to place my order. But the man there said they were all out of bread. And that was that. No more bread, so everyone must go home. I was disappointed.

The woman behind me smiled. She was an elderly lady with gray hair. She was very refined and nice-looking. She must have seen my disappointment and empathized. She said, "I know a baker where they have something guaranteed."

"I'm not supposed to go with anybody."

But she convinced me to go with her. The baker was a whole train stop away. We walked together. I made sure not to take her hand and insisted that we walk on opposite sides of the sidewalk. I didn't want her to get close to me. I was not supposed to go with strangers, after all. It was getting dark, and the street traffic was heavy. We walked for forty-five minutes before we arrived there. It was in a part of town I had seen before by the next train stop. It was just a regular storefront. When we arrived at the baker's, he was also out of bread. I was very depressed by this news. But she said she knew of another place where they would find bread. I listened and followed her to the next bakery. This time, it turned out that the baker was actually closer to my home. And so we walked back in the direction of my apartment, still keeping the sidewalk between us. At this bakery, she walked up to the counter and demanded, "Give this little child a whole loaf of white bread and half a loaf of black."

I heard what she said, but by this point I was so exhausted I didn't even say that the order was wrong. I was happy just to have the bread. I wanted to take it and go home. We got the bread and went out into the street. There, the nice lady said that she would help me carry the bag home. But I was suspicious.

"I can carry it on my own."

But she said, "No, it's not a problem. I will take one side of the bag, and you take the other. I just don't want it to be too heavy for you."

She did just that and we walked along the dark street in tandem, passing many ruins in the darkness. I thought to myself, "If she tries anything now, I can run away. I know my way around here."

When we got to my building, she said goodbye to me and walked away. I went indoors and up the stairs with the bag to show my parents what I had brought. By this point, several hours had passed, and they were in a panic. They had already gone down to the baker to look for me, but no one had seen a thing.

"Where have you been?" my mother asked.

I reached into the bag to show them. I pulled out just the half loaf of black bread. The lady took the loaf of white. She must have really needed it. My father approached me. He gave me a real spanking. Then he sent me to bed. I got no dinner. That was the only time that happened. Even if he had to go hungry, I got fed.

In an hour, Mom came into the room. She was holding some of the bread.

"No, I'm not hungry," I said. I was sobbing. I didn't think I'd done anything wrong. After all, I had never let the woman touch me. I even walked on the other side of the sidewalk. I couldn't help it if she stole from me. I just wanted to succeed and get food for everyone.

My mother was working in the flower shop then. My father helped her buy this shop with the aid of his uncle. Now they devoted a good deal of their time to getting the shop off the ground.

I guess there was a strong market for flowers in the rebuilding phase. People really wanted little luxuries and beautiful things, even though food was so short. Sometimes something beautiful can make all the difference.

The Russians were making it very difficult to bring food and supplies into West Berlin. Only a trickle of what the West sent got past the Russians, who would hold up supply trains for days or not allow them to come in at all. The Russians believed they could irritate the West into cutting Berlin loose. This was before the Soviets decided to entirely blockade the city.

I went with the other kids from around our apartment to the train station, where we waited for the locomotive drivers to throw down briquettes, which we scrambled to grab and bring home to heat our ovens. In Berlin we had it very hard. Even The Tiergarten, which was like New York's Central Park and close to the Reichstag and the Brandenburg Gate, was completely free of any trees. They were all chopped down to use for heating.

CHAPTER 8

Kleinmachnow

I wanted to be in school. The city was still in rubble but that didn't stop Germans from having school, and I wanted to be there. I was only five. For some reason I believed that my mother would forget to enroll me. She was so busy with the new flower shop that this was a possibility in my mind. She promised several times that she would. I kept asking her to make sure. She would say that of course she was going to enroll me when the time came.

I didn't want to take any chances so I decided to enroll myself. I only had an inkling where the school was when I began walking there. Later in the day I was supposed to go to my grandparent's house. I knew my way around the city well and thought I would be home in time to make the train out from Berlin. Besides, I was taking the trip by myself this time to Kleinmachnow. Mom said it was okay. I had been telling her that I could do it for a little while now. I wasn't going to miss the opportunity to prove myself.

I asked people that I passed in the streets if they knew where the school was. That's how I made it there. The school didn't even have a name at that point. It was simply named after the street it was on. Berlin was in terrible shape. Many of the buildings were large piles of rubble, or there was only the standing façade with nothing behind it. Every piece of stone and brick seemed to have been chipped by bullets. Some months had passed since the battle for Berlin ended. By this point, the bodies had been cleaned up at least, but there were still many strange smells. In old photos of the time, Berlin looks like the end of the world. And it did then, too, but as a little girl I could have fun there within the bombed-out city. With my parents and other relatives so involved in the flower shop, they didn't have much time for a child who wasn't in school. And I often was left to go about on my own, especially before school started. It was a very different time. You didn't have to worry about people stealing children—maybe just their bread.

When I reached the school, I found that the Allies had bombed it. A substantial portion of the building was missing. But I could see that there were still people working inside, and there were children already attending class. Outside, they teased me. Kids are very cruel. They saw that I was alone, and that I was small, and that I wasn't already enrolled with them, so they began taunting me a little.

I waited until they all went back in. The school was large, made of brick, and old. Part of it was missing, and there were black soot marks on the façade. It was not welcoming. I walked through the doors. Inside were these wide, big stairs. I felt small beneath them, but I climbed right up, step by step. At the top, an adult came up and said, "What are you doing here? Are you in a class?"

"No, not yet. But I want to be. I want to see the director."

"Oh, really," she said. "And where is your mother?"

"My mother is very busy. She can't come."

The woman smiled and led me to the director's office. She told the director what she knew.

"Oh, I understand. So . . . what is your name?"

I told her my name. I gave her my age and then said, "I am supposed to go to school here, and I want to register."

"That's good," she said, "But it would help if we could talk with your mother. We might get some more information from her."

"I just want to make sure that she doesn't miss out and that I am going," I said.

She then told me not to worry, that I was registered, but I should bring my mother back. I left the school feeling so happy walking through the streets, but I must not have been paying attention because I got lost. It took me an hour to get home. This was the summer of 1946, just prior to my sixth birthday.

At home, nobody seemed to have noticed that I disappeared for several hours. My mother and my aunt must have just assumed I was playing outside. And I think my mother had some confidence in me, too. But I didn't tell her about enrolling for class. That was just insurance. Instead, I went straight into asking about the train, which I had been looking forward to taking alone all day long. I wanted to show I could do it myself. I liked going to my grandparent's house.

It was an adventure for a little girl, even though it was only twelve miles or so away. I would have to take two separate trains. We had done it so much that it wasn't a problem for me. I didn't need my parents to hold my hand. Mom helped me prepare for the train. Dad said "bye" to me at the door, and I left. I walked out to the street and headed to the station, which was just a few blocks from the house. As I rounded the corner onto the next block, I saw my mother stalking me. I pretended not to notice her. She was checking to see if I really could do it. And since I wanted to prove it to her, I kept right on going. I headed to the Lichterfelde West train station. When the Metro train pulled in with all its noise and automatic doors, I got on and left. After a few stops, we arrived at the Zehlendorf Mitte station, where I met the other departing train. I made the switch with no problem.

At the station in Kleinmachnow, I waited for my grandfather. He picked me up there, which was a trend that he began that day. It was a very long walk. I think he liked to take the walk. And he liked to pick up his granddaughter. We had fun. He held my hand. I talked about the things I had done and seen. I told him of the school, and of my friends.

He listened to me. But it was preparation for his storytelling. That's the time I really waited for anyhow. Even when my parents were with us, the thing I looked forward to most was when my grandfather told me his stories. There was no television at my grandparents'. For that matter, there was no television in our apartment in Berlin. But the way my grandfather, Opi, told stories was better than television. As he spoke, I saw every word.

I waited for this the entire week in Berlin. He'd place me on his lap and tell me tales of Africa, and many other lands. It was no different this weekend, except this was the first time my parents didn't also make the trip out to Kleinmachnow with me. From now on, I could do it on my own. This gave them the chance to be alone for the weekend, but

I certainly wasn't just shunted off to the grandparents. It was the place I wanted to go.

When the weekend was over, Opi walked me all the way back to the train station. He talked to me all the way there. At the station, he gave me a little kiss and sent me on my way. My mother was waiting for me in Berlin. She was very happy to see me. At five years old, I proved to her that I could safely take two trains on my own. Of course no one would let her children do such a thing now; it was a different world then.

In the morning, my mother took time off to enroll in the school. We walked hand in hand to the building where I had been just days before, although my mother took a much more direct route than I had. When we arrived, she walked straight into the main offices and asked about enrolling me. They, in turn, led us into the director's office. The director smiled when she saw me and said, "Hello, Thea."

"Hello."

"How do you know each other?" my mother asked.

"Thea was here before asking about enrolling herself."

My mother finished the enrollment, and we left. On the way home she didn't mention the fact that I had tried to enroll myself at the school. We just walked along. Most of the rubble had been pushed off the roads and into neat piles that stood on the vacant lots of the bombed-out buildings. But this didn't concern me now. What did concern me was that because of bomb damage at the school, I would only be able to attend this week during the afternoons. They operated on an alternating schedule. Half the school came in the mornings and the other half in the afternoon, and then they switched. I really couldn't wait to take the full day of study instead of just half, and I wondered when they would finally be done fixing the place.

I happily took up the challenge of going to school and of walking there on my own, which to me was a very simple enterprise. On my route home, I often passed a large apartment complex that was surrounded by barbed wire. This was one of the American bases in Berlin. Whenever I walked, I liked to sing to myself. One time as I was singing and passing by the barbed wire fence, a G.I. was leaning out of the fence and shouting, "Stop! Stop!" All the children in my school had started to speak our first words of English, so I could communicate with this American soldier in some way.

I said, "Okay, but I'm not going to come in there."

"You can't come in, anyway. This is barbed wire."

I stopped walking and went over by the barbed wire. He told me to wait and then went inside the building and came out with his arms full of chocolate, candy, and chewing gum. He handed these treasures through the wire fence. There were so many pieces of candy I could barely carry them all. I had both my little hands around this package, pressing it to my chest for dear life. I knew I couldn't eat this before bringing it home to my family. And so I thanked the young G.I., who seemed very happy to have given me all this candy, and walked back to my house. There, my father was nearly as happy as I had been to get the chocolate. My father asked, "Where did you get that?"

When I told him the story, he said, "Well, whenever we are in need of chocolate, you could always just go and walk by that building."

I was proud that I was able to bring back so much candy and chocolate to my family. Food was so short that these gifts from the Americans played very well with the beleaguered Germans. It goes to show how powerful a piece of propaganda being kind can be.

CHAPTER 9

Opi

For the whole train ride out, I looked forward to telling Opi about how the American G.I. had given me all that candy, and how Daddy had said that if the family needed chocolate they could just send me out to get it.

When I arrived at Kleinmachnow, he was smiling and waiting for me. We greeted each other and began our walk back to the house. I couldn't wait and told him about what I had done that week. He listened as he always did. It was so pleasant there.

When I arrived at the house, Omi had food waiting for us. She plied me with questions, and I eventually told her the same stories of my week in Berlin as I had told Opi on the walk over. Sometimes he would chime in with little facts he had picked up from my story.

Later in the evening after we ate, we went onto the enclosed porch. That's where he told his stories. This had been the way it worked for some time. My grandmother would be in the kitchen just around the corner while my grandfather would tell me stories.

Opi walked to his desk and pulled out his big calendar book, which had stories from Africa and wonderful pictures. I could spend hours just looking at those pictures. There were animals I had never seen and strange people and lands that were so different from Germany. He put me on his lap and began telling me the stories. He started by reading from the calendar book. He often did this, and then when the reading jogged his memory, he shifted to remembering his own experiences. He talked of the time before the First World War when he had been stationed in colonial German South-West Africa. This was in the time of the German Empire. It was romantic. He had adventures then. And the people he described were so small. He told me of the Pygmies he knew from the Post where he was stationed. Apparently they were very friendly to him. He liked them because they were so small. He said I was small like they were—maybe they were a little bigger, or at least the women were very small like me. Then he began to touch me. I didn't know what he was doing, not at six. But he wasted no time. He was between my legs and hurting me in a short period. My grandmother was just in the kitchen, maybe two meters away beyond the wall.

He saw I was hurt. "Don't say anything. Don't say anything," he said.

"Opi, Opi. You are hurting me."

What was this he was doing? He stopped. He seemed nervous. I thought he was examining me like a doctor. This made sense. And I told him he could examine me if that's what he was doing, because that's the only time someone looked there if there was a problem, but I had no problem. He could examine just so long as he didn't hurt me any longer. He stopped telling his story then.

The house was dark when we returned inside. We said nothing. But it was later now and near time for bed. My grandparents slept in different rooms. She slept in the bedroom in a regular bed. And he slept in another room, which he had reconstructed since the bomb fell. In there, he had a pullout bed.

That night he wanted me to sleep together with him. This was not an unusual request and was one I typically granted without reserve. Tonight was no different. I thought we had played a game on the porch. One that hurt for a moment, but a game nevertheless, and now it was over and we could go back. But in the night in the darkness in the bed, he went further. He wasn't wasting time. And I thought that he had gone to the bathroom. I didn't know what he had done. He told me to be silent. He made sure I was silent. I didn't make a noise. This was the beginning.

The house at Kleinmachnow had several out buildings in the rear. There was no indoor plumbing, so we had an outhouse. We also had a washing kitchen, some ways off from the back of the house, where the dishes were done. But this washing kitchen was large. My grandparents used it for storage. They kept many of their old things in there. This meant there was a horde of toys for me.

Right after the war we had very little. So many people had lost everything that the old material comforts were hard to come by. Since our apartment was burned to the ground I had no toys left at all, just whatever my parents were able to pick up in the aftermath. Even my Peter doll was destroyed. To me, that washing kitchen was a wonderful place. It was the closest thing to a toy store that I would see for a while, or that I even ever remember seeing. Opi knew this. When my grandmother recalled that she had a pair of roller skates back there, Opi volunteered to take me.

"I will get them for you, but you have to touch Opi first."

No longer was the washing kitchen a place I looked at with wonder. I wanted nothing to do with it because of what he had done there. It was in that small outbuilding where he said that if I told anyone about what he had done, he would have me arrested. He knew the police, and because I was such a wicked little girl, they would be sure to send me away to the jail. You will believe such things when you are just a little child. I didn't know how false what he said was, and I was afraid to say anything about what he did to me to anyone. But I had trouble keeping secret the things he had done, despite what I thought the consequences would be.

It continued this way. I quickly stopped wanting to go to my grandparents' house and stopped going by myself all together. Whenever there was any question that my parents might send me out to Kleinmachnow, I found reasons not to go. I either didn't feel well, or there was something I needed to do for school.

We still went there together as a family from time to time. Opi was very nice to me then. He always looked for ways to get alone with me. On one occasion, he took me aside and brought me candy. Later he told me that he was the one who stole the cheese. By this point, the cheese was the least of my worries. Nevertheless, it troubled me to know that he ate the cheese, that I lied about what I hadn't done, and that he could send me to jail when he was hurting me.

I don't know if my mother was suspicious, or if anyone had any idea what happened. I know that my grandmother didn't know. But at school, what happened became a problem for me. I could no longer keep it a secret. I still really believed he would send me off to prison if I told anyone.

In the bathroom one day with a group of other schoolmates, I shouted out what my grandfather had done. Someone took me seriously because before too long my mother brought me to the doctor. She believed me enough to try to find out if what I said was true. The doctor was very friendly to me. She began the examination immediately. I was not happy with her doing this to me, even though she was a doctor. Had it not have happened, of course, I might have felt differently. I justified what Opi had done as a doctor's exam. Now the real thing had undertones of the violation.

When she finished examining me, she kept me waiting while she talked with my mother. Then she very kindly shook my hand goodbye, and we left. My mother was quiet as we walked back to our Berlin apartment. She did, however, acknowledge that the doctor confirmed what I said. She would never again leave me alone with him. She stopped taking us out there almost altogether. My dad, on the other hand, refused to believe that his own father would do this to his granddaughter. "I would kill him if I thought that was true," he said. Even with this, he didn't protest when my mother ceased going to his parents' house.

My mother later told me that when she confronted Opi with what he had done, he tried to say that I was blackmailing him. He said that because he gave me candy one day, and never again, I was doing this to retaliate. In other words, I was lying to punish him for not giving me more candy. I don't know whether or not he said this before or after my mother had brought me to the doctor. I just know that my mother told me later this was how he defended himself against the accusation.

CHAPTER 10

Surrogate Family

It's always the same. I'm walking on a street in the outskirts of Berlin, and there are holes everywhere. I jump over one and another, but before too long I fail to reach the pavement on the other side. I fall in and continue falling and falling. There's no bottom. I never hit one, nor do I ever see the bottom. I just fall and fall, and then I am awake and back home in our small apartment in Berlin. My family lives here with my Uncle Karl and his daughters, my cousins. I like living in a family group like this. Many people complain about being on top of each other, but as a little child I find it fun.

With all those people I never have to be alone. There's always someone to talk with, or I'm in school. But when I sleep, I'm alone. That's when the nightmares come. I have these dreams all the time—falling through the holes. One night I am so terrified I wet the bed. I am so embarrassed. This is not what older girls do. But I have done it.

I show my mom what I have done. I feel ashamed, but my mom does not punish me. When I was very small and wet the bed, my mother would show at least some displeasure. But now, she says nothing. She merely changes the sheets. I think she has a suspicion about what's causing me to behave in this way and so she let's this pass. She is very kind to me, my mom.

I was eight years old. That's when we learned there was a chance that I could live with a surrogate family. My school was offering children the opportunity to go live with foster parents in the West. I told my dad about this program, and he checked it out. Then he said, "Yes, you can do it."

He would do anything so that I had enough. My dad was worried that he wouldn't be able to provide food for me under the present conditions. The Russians were blockading West Berlin. Our vast half of the city was landlocked within East Germany. The full ramifications of the Cold War hadn't played out yet, but it was obvious to my dad that I would be better taken care of in West Germany. As retaliation for consolidating the French, British, and American zones into one zone known as West Berlin, the Soviets blockaded the city from all outside supplies. The goal was to cut us off completely from the outside world until the Americans capitulated and handed the city over to the Soviets.

Food was scarce. We ate dried potatoes and carrots, which had to be flown in. Planes landed nearly every thirty seconds at the airport. The Soviets could not stop the air supply. But our lives were hard.

Under these conditions my father was happy to send me away. There was an application process. I had a lung problem at the time. This fact played a role in my getting awarded the honor of moving to the West with a new family. We received notification by mail. However, as an eight-year-old girl, moving to a small town north of Hamburg with people who were unfamiliar to me was not the greatest "honor" I could imagine.

Just before I left, I was walking with my mother outside our flower shop. Above us in the sky, I saw little pieces of tissue paper falling.

"Mommy, what's that?"

At first it was hard to tell what was happening, but then she said, "Those are little parachutes. Go get one." I waited in the street as they came down and grabbed one. Inside there was a little Hershey's bar. That morning I was not hungry. I had all the chocolate I could eat. Many people came into the streets to catch the falling chocolate. It was such a wonderful thing for the Americans to do. One man, the "Chocolate Bomber" Gail Halvorson, had decided to drop chocolate for the children as he was landing in Berlin. Then the Americans made a habit of doing it.

I left on a cargo flight one spring morning. My family came to see me off. It was somber. My dad acted in a cheerful way. He wanted me to know the opportunity I had before me. My mom, however, was unhappy to be losing her daughter to another family.

There were many little children who came that day to be sent away to the West. Their families all piled onto the runway to see them off. Many of the mothers felt like mine. You could tell from their faces. These were people who had endured the war and then the Russians. The family members remaining with them now were those who had lived through it all. And now they were sending their precious children away.

We were all put on cargo planes. Little did I know how familiar I would become with this sort of travel later in life. I caught a glimpse of my mother as the plane taxied down the runway, and then the plane was flying. Inside the hold, we were bombarded by noise and wind. We flew to Lübeck in the north near Hamburg. The city is old and charming, famous for making the almond paste known as marzipan. The flight was not too long but uncomfortable. The British flew the planes. The planes were the transports from the Berlin Airlift. They must have figured since these flights were empty on their return to the West, they should use them to help take out whatever children they could. In 1948, the city looked much as it did the day after the war. How could rebuilding go on under the first squeeze by the Soviets and then under the blockade? Except for the Berlin Brick Ladies who stacked bricks from the ruins for later rebuilding, very little happened to the city's landscape in those years.

When we landed at Lübeck, they put signs around our little necks with our names on them. Then the adults who corralled us put us onto trains. In this kind of herd, you don't know where you are going. The place is unfamiliar and you just follow what people are saying. I know I had to switch trains. But how I did it I can't recall. I was eight years old and changing trains was like rolling over in bed for me. My foster parents were at the platform, waiting. They recognized me by the sign on my neck. They were very happy. The foster mother quickly took the sign off me. It made me seem like a piece of merchandise.

As soon as I arrived I began missing my family. I especially missed my cousins and my mom. The people I was there to live with were kind to me. I did learn, too. But it was a little different there in school. They were still hitting kids. The teachers would check under your fingernails. If they weren't exactly clean, or they found a little black there, the ruler came down on your hands.

I was well fed by my foster family. We always had milk, which was special to me since milk had been so hard to come by in Berlin. The family I was with could not have kids themselves, so I became like a daughter to them. From my perspective, I did not look to them as replacements for my parents, but I did have an affection toward them. And I was happy to be going to school. I was even a little ahead.

I took a negative view of myself then. The old Thea sill remained: the little girl who knew what she wanted and walked through Berlin to enroll herself at school, only to be blunted by a growing sense of inferiority and ugliness.

My surrogate parents were kind to me. They helped me along, but my mom had grown to miss me. I had been gone for ten months. I was terribly homesick. My mom decided she couldn't stand it anymore and wrote that she was coming to see me. In order to get to me, she had to go through the Eastern Zone. Of course, she wasn't allowed to go there. There's no telling what the Russians would have done if they found her. She would have been jailed at the least.

She found a group of people who were leaving to the West through the Eastern Zone. They were doing what they called a "black border crossing." Russians and East Germans heavily guarded the border. She took a train that got her into the East and as close to the Western border as she could get. They didn't call us "islanders" for nothing. Then she and the group ran through the forest. They could see border guards where they were standing by a road that marked West Germany. They were careful and quiet among the trees and shrubs. Once they reached the West, they all found transportation and went their separate ways. My mom caught a train north, to Hamburg, and she came to see me.

When she walked up to the house, I couldn't believe it was her. Ten months to a child is like a decade to an adult. I said, "Mutti, Mutti, I have to go back with you."

But she couldn't take me. "This is way too dangerous," she said. She wasn't going to bring me on a black border crossing, which would have been a risk to both of us. But she promised that she would get me out very soon. The foster parents were not happy, but they understood. The scene before their eyes, I'm sure, was heartfelt. How could they say no? I couldn't stand to be separated from my mom again. Leaving her for this family was one thing, but having her come and go was another thing altogether. I was upset. I didn't want her to go.

When she left, she promised again that she would come back for me. "I'll find a way, somehow," she said. Then she took a dangerous trip back to West Berlin through the Eastern Zone. She made it back through the same forest and onto a train. My mom had a lot of nerve to go through that border for her daughter as she did. But she was as sick at heart as I was.

A few months passed. By this point I had been with my foster parents about a year. After my mother left I was just sick to myself. I only wanted to go home to her. In Berlin, they devised a plan to get me. My Uncle Karl worked for the railroad. Because of his job, he had a special pass that allowed him to go through the zones.

He came to the house where I was living. They had made arrangements with my foster family. I was elated when I saw him. "Uncle Karl," I said, "I'm so happy to see you." After giving me a big hug, he sat down and said, "Look, from now on you don't call me Uncle Karl, you call me Daddy."

"Yes, Uncle Karl."

"No, not Uncle Karl. You call me Daddy."

"Yes, Uncle Karl." He didn't think I was as funny as I did. Then he made me practice calling him "Daddy." Of course, I wasn't going to make the mistake of calling him Uncle Karl, but he was afraid. Once he felt satisfied that I would not call him Uncle Karl in public, we got ready to go to the train. But my foster parents were very upset to see me go. They had bonded with me, and since they couldn't have children, I was their little daughter. But the time had come. It just wasn't going to work out. My family wanted me back too much, and I wanted to be back home. Leaving was sad, though. Uncle Karl said to them, "She is too homesick. She has to go. And her parents can't stand it, either."

He thanked them. We left. My foster parents didn't make the separation any worse than it needed to be. There was no scene at their house. At that train station, however, it was a different story. Uncle Karl took me to the station. He was sweating. This got worse when we boarded the train and the East German soldiers began walking up and down checking passports. They were very thorough. They checked each and every person on that train for their papers. We watched as they moved closer to us. By the time they got to us, Uncle Karl was shaking he was so nervous.

The soldiers came by, and he gave them his passport. They motioned to me. Karl said, "This is my daughter. She is too young to have a passport."

The soldiers examined his passport further and looked at me. I just smiled and said, "Yes, Daddy. Yes, Daddy." The soldiers then moved on down the train. After that, we had no more trouble, and Uncle Karl stopped sweating. I was just a little girl. I had little concept of what they might do. Who knows what it would have been? If they were willing to send a little girl away into Russia during the occupation, then maybe they would have done something to me. People were certainly jailed all the time, and for reasons you might have never heard or even understood.

Once we entered our island of West Berlin, we no longer had to worry about what the Russians may do to us. We got to my apartment in no time. My family was happy to see me. My mother hugged me. And my father had organized five large pears as a homecoming gift. Pears were very hard to get then. We didn't get candy; the only way we got that was if the Americans dropped Hershey bars down with parachutes. I was happy with the pears.

My dad was a pretty good businessman. He was at least good at acquiring luxury items in blockaded Berlin and selling them for a profit. He once got oranges in a box. But the oranges came wrapped in a type of gold foil. Some of the gold had rubbed off onto the oranges and made them sparkle. He saw that and went about rubbing all the gold foil off onto the oranges so that they sparkled like some kind of golden orange. He sold them from our shop as exactly that: bona fide golden oranges. And people paid for them.

The Russians really thought they could break us with this blockade, or that they could shake the Americans into letting the city become totally controlled by them. But they never let it go. The Americans basically said, "Over our dead body. You're not going to get Berlin." The Americans wanted us on their side. In May of 1949, the Americans ran the blockade. By treaty, they had the right to access their sector of the city, so they did. They assembled an entire column of tanks and Jeeps and rode through the Eastern Zone toward Berlin.

It was a huge column, and they ran the blockade. The Soviet soldiers or the East German soldiers stood down when they saw it. They must not have known what to do. Nobody wants to be the soldier who starts a shooting war between two great powers.

The column came right by where my uncle and aunt were. My uncle had never considered himself a great friend of the Americans. But when they came he went outside and picked flowers from a field. He walked up to the G.I.s and said, "Welcome to Berlin." We really knew at that point that the Americans weren't going to let us go. But remaining isolated in Berlin as we were, even without the blockade, was not going to work for us forever, at least not for my father.

CHAPTER 11

The West

"Passports," the East German soldier said.

Mom and Dad handed them over. Mom smiled. Dad nodded. The train sat on tracks headed for West Germany, which was only a hundred meters away. The East German soldiers were grim in their drab uniforms. I despised them. They were worse than the Russians.

I handed my passport to the man in uniform as rudely as possible. I would not look at him. I acted like he was a contagious germ, not to be touched. Nor did I make a sound. I held the papers above my head. He took them in a swift motion—the same motion by which he would arrest me if he could. He handed the papers back. I took them the same way I had given them and stuffed them into my bag like trash. They should know how much they disgusted me, I thought.

My mom felt otherwise. She was upset by my act. These East German soldiers frightened her. She knew very well what they were capable of. And she thought it was silly and unnecessary to rattle their cage, and of course dangerous. The East German soldier before us now was the same sort of man who had sent her to a labor camp near the Baltic to dig ditches. All because a zealous Nazi neighbor overheard her say something to the effect that she would not attend the party rally because she couldn't stand that idiot Hitler.

It took months of attempts by family who were either party members in good standing, or commissioned officers in the army, to set her free. As a twelve-year-old girl, I had no such direct experience of a local authority with power over life and death. I had seen the invasion, of course, but this was a special case; it's different when your own police arrest you for something you've said. And it's different when your own youthful skepticism toward authority actually gets you sent away. I had never known the feeling of total helplessness that this engenders, and she didn't want me to find out.

She was not going to fool with these soldiers. The East Germans had taken to their totalitarian roles with glee. They were prepped for it under the Nazis and made the transition to the Soviet system without a hiccup. This may speak volumes as to their compatibility. But how and why they were what they were didn't matter to me. What mattered was how they behaved.

We moved to Frankfurt in 1952. My father was looking to better his career. I think this was also the time that Opi stopped molesting me, only because we no longer saw him as much. I later learned that he did not cease doing this kind of thing: he kept right on going with my cousins. The move would make our family life easier. Frankfurt was the economic center of Germany then. Berlin, because of its position in the East, was now isolated. However, getting back in and out of the city was easier than it had been before. We had special West Berlin passports that allowed us to travel. The blockade was no more, and the Soviets agreed to give the West Berliners some freedom of movement. In other words, we could leave. They had abandoned their hope of uniting the city under Soviet rule, at least by blockade. Those on the other side of the line had no such papers. They were trapped. The greatest hang-up with respect to soldiers and borders we now encountered was having to endure brisk passport checks on the train. Of course, something terrible could always happen at this point, especially if you mistreated these soldiers or questioned their authority. But for the most part, we were outside of their reach now.

To be trapped on one side of the line or the other was almost a matter of accident, based on where the Allies made the demarcation when the war ended. However, my father knew enough to move us to the West when it was possible to do so. So there was also an element of wit and wisdom, which got people on either the East or West side of the Berlin dividing line. I wouldn't say that West Berliners carried a sense of superiority, but a sense of being in a better position. Of course, there were those Easterners who believed in the Soviet system.

For them I felt little affection. But most Easterners would have preferred to be in the West. And the city was not truly closed until Nikita Khrushchev made the suggestion on the night of August 12, 1961. He saw that the open border was a drain on human material. That night, the East Germans strung up thirty miles of barbed wire. Construction of the Wall began immediately.

Since the end of the war, the East Germans were considerably poorer than we were. My Uncle Karl blamed their plight not on Socialism, but on what he called Stalinistic Fascism. He said, "They don't have Socialism. They don't even know what Socialism is."

I used to dream that a bell would ring, and we would all be very happy. That was it for the dream: a bell and happiness. But like all dreams, this had a texture and a context. It had to do with my family, our lives, and the discontinuity of the division.

My father made more money in Frankfurt. We rented a place from a farmer thirty minutes by train into the country. Now we had more room than we ever had in Berlin. For a city girl, the move was startling. The farm was lovely, but I missed all the people. And I was separated from my cousins. As I got older, I took the train back to visit them whenever I could on the weekends. But at first, I felt isolated.

There was no local high school. The town was too small. I had to travel by bus to the new school, which was regional. At the school, they blended the classical and modern German educations. This meant that we were taught English, Latin, and French with some Greek thrown in. In modern schools of the time, you would learn French and English. The classical schools taught Latin and Greek. This place was a fusion of the two.

When I graduated from high school, I was offered an opportunity to attend the University of Frankfurt to be an Economics teacher on a scholarship. But my family could not afford to pay any part of the housing and expenses. They needed me to do something where I could take care of myself. They could no longer afford to take care of me. I therefore declined the scholarship.

I might have defied my mother had I felt that I deserved good things, but I retained a nagging sense of inferiority. This sense was only tempered and often overwhelmed by my Prussian sense of purpose. These two aspects made for a bi-polar mixture within me: a sense of shame and inferiority, which I had been taught, and a sense of purpose and achievement that, I think, must have been inborn. When I think of my cousin Helmut at sixteen leading his remaining family away from the invaders, I imagine the drive is hereditary.

One of my greater embarrassments in high school is tangled with this sense of shame and purpose. In English class, I had a teacher who did not care for me. But I liked English. I thought it was important for me to speak it well. I also thought that I did speak it well and that I understood it. However, on the final paper I received an "F" because the teacher did not like my writing. This was the only time I received an "F" in any class. This hurt me. The teacher was certainly cruel and grading me unfairly; however, I did nothing about it. I remained silent. The grade at once confirmed my ugly suspicions of my self and drove me to learn English.

After high school, my father enrolled me in a three-year business apprenticeship comprised of equal parts practical work and formal schooling. The practical work consisted of apprenticeship at a factory that made typewriters. I cycled through all the departments there, from accounting to sales and so on. There was not a single job that I ever considered doing. The only part of my time there that was at all memorable was the time I spent writing. Of course, I used one of the typewriters that we manufactured. I would sit at my desk in one of the departments and write stories of Africa. I would just make them up out of whole cloth. A few times I showed managers my work, but they were never impressed.

I finished the program in two and a half years. Even though the program was run so that they retain their apprentices, I wanted no part of this job. Many children just graduating find themselves in a place where they cannot stand the options in front of them. I determined to do something about it. Rather than take the job which awaited me at the end of the factory program, I chose to leave the program early and learn English. I was still stung by the "F" I had received from that frivolous teacher.

I thought, "God damn it, I'm going to show her that I can learn English."

I also resolved to get out of Germany. I found an advertisement for an agency, which arranged au pairs for families in London. I went for an interview and was hired. Soon thereafter, I headed to Great Britain.

In my new job I did not have to raise children, as is the case with most au pairs. The children of the family I was assigned to were my age or older. But I had to take care of the couple. The husband was blind, and his wife was dying of cancer. I thought, in my pride, she can't die on my watch.

My first duty at the house was to cook a Sunday roast. I had never cooked a roast before and had very little experience in cooking whatsoever. The only direction I had was that the meat should be rare. I took the roast, patted it with salt and pepper, placed it inside a pan in the oven, and began to cook it. What temperature I cooked it at I can't be sure, but I was so concerned about getting it right that I cut into that meat and stabbed it so often it was barely recognizable as a roast when I was finished. He never complained though. I thought, "Well, I can't be worse than the British cooks." But I was a little ashamed about my inexperience with cooking a roast.

Being an au pair was not bad work. I was safe for the most part, and they were very kind to me. The work was easy. I learned English quite well. We talked often. And I think he took a sort of pride in my advancement in the language. I also spent a good deal of time reading English. I went to a school and got my proficiency in the language, which consisted of both an oral and written exam.

I envisioned moving back to Frankfurt and showing that wicked English teacher that I could speak the language better than she could. I never did that, though. When I returned from London and could speak well enough, I thought it would be childish to go. After about three months in the U.K., I started dreaming in English, and when my mother came to visit me after about seven months, I sat her down in the kitchen and told her all about my life there and what I was doing in English. She just stared at me and let me go on. Then she said, "Hello, I am Mutti, and I speak German." I didn't even get it for a few seconds.

But all that was still to come. In London, I began to search out a social life. The difficulty of doing this, however, was the family I lived with in High Barnet. At that time, it was the last stop on the tube, and you still had to take a bus. I got a job working behind the bar at a club that played live music. I fell madly in love with the violinist. I used to wait for him, hoping he would take me home. Not that I planned to go to bed with him. I was not like that. But I wanted to be closer to him. It was also true that my commute home was horrible. I had to walk to the tube, where I traveled several stops, only to take a bus. From there, I had to walk almost a mile to my home. On one side of the road were houses that were set back, and on the other side was a very large field. The walk was somewhat desolate. In other words, I really could have used a lift back home for the sake of convenience and safety.

One night, a man followed me from the train to the bus. It was very dark. I did not see that he then followed me off the bus as well. But as I began walking I could tell someone was behind me. I began walking faster. I got near my home, and the man jumped me. I cried out in German. Then I realized that no one would understand me.

The man was very strong. I couldn't do anything. I tried to get loose, but he dragged me by the neck to the side of the road. He pulled me into the drainage ditch and covered my mouth in the dirt and weeds. Then he looked around to see if anyone had heard me scream. He sat on my chest in the ditch with his head up, looking out into the field and back again to the houses. I thought he was going to kill me. I was afraid, but I did not act like it. I made eye contact with him and lay perfectly still and somehow communicated that I would not scream. I could not talk because he covered my mouth.

He released his grip. I said, "What do you want?"

"I want to meet you."

"This is the way you do it? You could have just come up and asked me for my name." He didn't say anything.

"Where did you see me?"

"I saw you in the tube, and you were so pretty."

I convinced him that we should get out of the ditch. I told him that we could talk at my house. When we climbed up onto the roadway, he was still holding onto me, but he was not holding my neck. I just kept talking and asking him questions. I found out he was an Irishman and that he sat across from me on the tube. When he released his hold, I ran away. I reached the door and rang the bell. My blind host came and answered. His first words were, "What's wrong?"

He brought me inside and called the police. I was shaken. He had nearly killed me when he choked me. Later, I was struck by the thought that I had talked my way out of that terrible situation. My confidence grew from this fact. However that may sound, it's true. A man was going to hurt me, and I stopped him from doing it by talking to him. I think this changed my whole attitude toward myself or at least put the change in motion. In school, I used to think, "Every other girl is prettier than me. Every other girl is smarter than me." However wrong this sentiment might have been, I couldn't shake it. Even later, in Vietnam, if a man told me I was beautiful, I knew he was lying.

I once asked a girlfriend of mine in high school whether she thought I had nice legs or not. "I think they're nice," I said. She didn't say anything then, but she told some of her friends, and the next day they started bullying me. "Oh, your legs are so gorgeous, Thea. See how gorgeous they are." From that point on, I knew never to share how I felt with anyone. "You're not going to do that again," I thought, but I also stopped fighting for myself. I didn't say anything back to those girls, nor did I say anything to the English teacher who had failed me with little reason. But when a man attacked me, I was able to persuade him into letting me go. I didn't lose my head. I talked to him. And I knew that I could keep my head this way if I was in a dangerous position again.

The man disappeared, but the police caught him not far from where he attacked me. I had to go to his trial and testify against him. They gave him six months in jail. At the end of the six months, I was worried that he would come find me and kill me. He had never been in jail before. This was his first time. He might hold a grudge, and so I arranged to leave to go back home short of the time I was supposed to be in England.

After I was attacked, my dad could not stand to have me away from him anymore. He called me often to tell me I should come home. He even bribed me, saying he would buy me new clothes and take me shopping if I returned to Germany to see him. I didn't shop for clothes in London because I didn't have any money. I bought one dress, which I wore to the younger son's wedding. It cost five pounds, and that was a fortune for me. Today that would be about $100.

My mom came to see me after I was attacked. She was very happy that I was living away from home, and of course happy at how well I had learned English, though she would have preferred that I talked to her in the language that she spoke. She liked that I was living abroad and seeing the world. But the idea that this man would come back to hurt me won the day. In short order, and just before he was released from jail, I left the country. I had been in London just under twelve months. Aside from learning English there, I came away with an absolute fear of having anyone walk behind me. Even now, if that happens, the hair stands up on my neck.

Back home in Frankfurt, I anticipated moving to Paris. I had always wanted to see that city. My goal, as with English, was to learn the language. I never got an "F" in French to motivate me, but I still wanted to know it better. I had learned the language in school, but I wasn't speaking it well. I knew that the only way to really learn a language was to enter its culture. And the French seemed to have such a wonderful one. Even the Germans looked at the French in this sort of romantic light. Hitler gave orders to destroy Paris, but his General refused to do so.

My other goals were to escape Germany, to escape my dad's protective ways, and to escape the destiny I feared. On this track, I would become a secretary and a German housewife in no time. But I wanted more. I was driven to have more even though I couldn't articulate what the more I wanted was, nor did I think I deserved it. My failure to articulate my dreams, or to have a concrete one translatable into a career, was a reason why my dad was able to scuttle my plans of moving to Paris.

"Over my dead body." He wouldn't stand for another trip of mine. In his eyes, this was wasting time before I started something more substantial. "You're not twenty-one yet and as long as you're not, I say what you do, and you are staying. I can't bear it to let you go again."

I had already completed the business program and gone off to England. After what happened there, he just didn't want to let me go.

But he went around Frankfurt looking for open positions I might take up. He knew I had rejected the factory and its life, so he searched for office jobs that might be more palatable to me. I wouldn't do anything to look for a job. I wanted to go to Paris; I didn't want a job.

I told him, "I'm not going to go for it. I'm going to move to Paris."

My mother would have let me go.

"Paris is even worse than London. I'm not going to let her go to Paris. Who knows what will happen," he told her.

He found me a job at the German offices of Oppenheimer and Co. This was an American broker that had just opened a branch in Frankfurt. They had an opening there for a secretary who could speak

English. From there I could study, and if I passed the examinations, I would become a licensed broker. My father secured the interview. He even took me to it. I went because the job would allow me to use my English and gave me a link to America. I also thought that I would only work there for a while, and then I would move to Paris with or without my dad's consent.

CHAPTER 12

Oppenheimer & Co.

"I represent a fund, the Putnam Fund, and we're looking to buy up part of a private German bank." This was Oppenheimer and Co. partner Paul O'Neil talking. I had been with the company under a year. And while I was studying to become a broker, I was not yet twenty-one and so could not take the examination. He needed someone he could trust, fluent in German and English, to help him make the deal. Rudolf Münemann owned the bank. He made himself famous when he invented revolving credit, where he lent money for up to thirty-five years and then refinanced the loan with cheaper short-term credit that would continue making money as long as the short-term interest rate didn't go up.

I was very flattered that this American businessman wanted to include me in such a large deal. Two million at the time would be worth something like fourteen million in today's dollars. Paul O'Neil was a partner, and we had become friends. He was my mentor. But many of these Americans simply thought buying a drink for a Fräulein would get her to bed with them. On one occasion, later on down the line, an American businessman called and asked me to lunch.

"Yes, I'm free for lunch, where do you want to meet?"

"Paris," he said. "Go to the airport; there's a helicopter waiting to fly you there."

I told him that my lunch breaks weren't long enough to allow me to go to a café in Paris. He got the point. But Paul was not that way.

"What are we going to do?" I asked him.

"I have to do the negotiations, but obviously I need someone to translate. First of all, we're going to follow him. And if I ever get to meet him, you will just translate for me."

We followed him for a while. We traveled by helicopter, all in an effort to get Münemann to meet with us. Eventually we started strategizing while sitting in the bar of the Frankfurter Hof, a famous hotel across the street from Münemann's bank in Frankfurt. We sat in the lobby, waiting. He finally got the idea that we weren't going to give up and granted us a meeting.

When that happened, Paul and I had an intense session at our favorite bar. "I need to know what this guy might ask us. Why don't I ask you the questions he might ask, and you answer them?"

Paul agreed. We went to the bar and drank Scotch. I played the banker and Paul played himself, and I asked him questions. He answered them as if we were making the deal. This did the trick. I listened to him and how he was not hastily giving answers. He stopped and thought before he spoke. I later learned that this was a trick to appear thoughtful, and to give time to answer. This was the effect I wanted. Don't just spill out the answers like I've rehearsed them, but say them like I'm considering my words. Paul decided I could speak with Münemann on my own.

So I went into the meeting with this older banker alone. I was only twenty at the time. I had had a suit made so that I'd look older. It was a dark blue jacket and skirt, and I was wearing a turned-up black hat. The hat was like something from Madeline, the children's book character. It was in at that time. I don't know why I thought it would make me look older because it certainly didn't. I always looked much younger than my age and resented this, as I did so many of my features.

I went to his office and gave him the proposal.

We sat together with a member of his Board of Directors. He listened to me and then said, "Why in the world would I want to sell two million dollars worth of shares to you?" We sat together in one of the rooms of his plush suite.

This is how the negotiations started. I saw his tone as an opening and gave him my spiel in as thoughtful and unrehearsed a way as I could manage. This is at least the effect I tried to achieve. He smiled while I talked. I could tell he liked me. When I finished he said, "All right." But he made no commitments. I could see he was smiling. Whether he was pleased with my proposal or just thought it was funny to have such a young woman approach him with a serious business deal was beyond me. And I felt a bit foolish, so I assumed, as usual, that he saw me as a fool.

I went back to the bar and met with Paul. "What happened?" I couldn't give him a definitive answer, so I told him everything. I think Paul was encouraged. We continued to follow Münemann around Germany. He knew we were determined. I think he thought I was so funny because he was telling his whole Board about me at the time, a fact which only later got back to me.

Then out of the blue, he told one of his Board members to call me. He told him, "Bring that little child in again. She is very funny. Let's hear what she comes up with next."

I went to meet with him again. There, I said things to him that no one else would say, like "What if something happens to you? You've got to diversify. What's going to happen to your daughter? Will the bank always be on top?" I had studied the man and knew a lot about him.

Our conversations went back and forth and back and forth. This went on for weeks. It wasn't done in a day. I got more confident every time we met. Then he finally said, "Okay, I promise you I will seriously think about this."

More time passed. He called the office. "Tell Miss Krieger I want her and her partner Paul O'Neill to come to my office. My Board and I will give you my decision."

We went to his bank. The secretary smiled and led us into the conference room. Inside were these high-backed chairs along the table. I felt so small. When I saw the chairs, I thought, "Oh, God." I turned to Paul and said, "I feel so silly sitting here like a little girl going to high tea with her Majesty the Queen. I don't know, maybe we've made fools of ourselves and they're going to laugh us out of town."

Mr. Münemann came in. He smiled. We smiled back. The Board members' faces were blank to me. Then Mr. Münemann said, "Please translate to Mr. O'Neill. You have a deal."

I turned to Paul and said, "We have a deal. We have a deal." We started shaking hands and congratulating ourselves. From that point forward, I believed I wanted to be a stockbroker. I thought that it was a really great way to make a living. You buy stocks. They go up, and you make money. Of course, the reality is more difficult than that.

My compensation for the deal was that Paul gave me a weekend trip to Berlin. That was it. I didn't complain. I liked working there. And I had only been an employee for a short time before Paul took me on the deal that I had no idea what I might have been entitled to. He took me in because my English was so good, and as a translator I was not a threat to Mr. Münemann. I don't think the fact that I was a twenty-year-old girl hurt me much in his consideration. Maybe Paul knew something about Münemann that he didn't tell me.

But I was happy in the position. I started taking classes with the Israeli spy who worked at Oppenheimer and Co. That's what we called him, anyway: the Mossad Agent. He was an Israeli man and a professor, and he was very cold and often cruel. German by birth, he became an Israeli citizen. Now he worked from this office. We just assumed he was a spy.

I was "only" a secretary, and he treated me poorly. But when he saw that I cared about the business and showed effort, he warmed up to me. He was helping to prep me for the certification test. You had to be twenty-one to take it in Germany, and I had to wait until August, 1961, for my birthday to pass.

I moved into a new apartment in Frankfurt, and my dad had to cosign the lease. My mom was enthusiastic about me living in my own place. She had married young when the war was on, so her life was somewhat constrained. The war years were terrible. And after the wedding, my dad left again. She was on her own with a newborn. She wanted me to see life and be as free as I could be.

At the University of Frankfurt, the classes mostly consisted of lessons I had already learned. It was all theoretical there, and I had already had daily practical lessons at Oppenheimer and Co. But I needed the certification. I went with another girl from the office to take the test. She failed. I passed. It was years later that she passed the test. Part of it consisted of memorizing every stock ticker symbol on the NYSE and American stock exchanges. This I did.

When I passed the second exam, I had a bright idea and went over to Münemann's bank. I told the secretary, "Would you please tell

Mr. Münemann that I am now a New York Stock Exchange broker—a fully registered representative?"

In return, I received a telegram from Münemann that came with a card and flowers. In those days you still received such things as telegrams. In the telegram, he congratulated me for my success. Of course I called him once I received the telegram. I asked him if he would give me some money to invest with. He did. He gave me 10,000 Marks, which, at that time, was a lot of money. I started investing. I thought this was an easier thing to do than it turned out. I had plenty of education and practical knowledge, but I didn't really do so well. Mr. Münemann may have been angry with me, but through my dad I heard about the Cuban Missile Crisis before almost any other civilian. I learned how serious it was from my father, who was working for the German Defense Ministry.

He said: "I want you to pack a suitcase and be ready to move on a moment's notice. I will tell you where you need to go."

I called up Münemann and told him about this. I told him he should be ready to get out. "This is very serious. We have a nuclear crisis on our hands."

But this was what saved my skin with him. I was starting to lose money at this point. And it became more and more clear to me that trading would not be my vocation.

Soon after I acquired certification, it came out in an economics newsletter that I was Germany's only female stockbroker and the youngest for the New York stock exchange. They wrote a big piece on it. At that point, I was attending a German American club. One night at the club, I met a man named Dick Rosenbaum. He asked a few questions. And since I was proud of what I had accomplished I was not shy about telling him that I was Germany's only, and youngest, certified stockbroker. He seemed impressed by this. He told me that he worked for American Forces Radio. At the time, this was Frankfurt's best radio station. On the weekends he produced a talk show on AFN called "Weekend World." It ran for two hours on both Saturday and Sunday. He invited me to join him the following week to discuss with one of the hosts what it was like to be Germany's only female stockbroker. Even now, being the "first" or the "only" will get you an interview.

Of course I agreed. I hardly remember the interview now. But I do remember feeling happy yet ironic that someone wanted to interview me at all. What I took away from the interview was a relationship with Dick. He was an American G.I. stationed in Germany. He was a journalist and had loved radio since a very young age. I think he started spinning records at a local station at the age of twelve. His other claim to fame, of course, was the Beatles. As a producer at AFN in Frankfurt, he selected who was played and interviewed. Dick turned down the Beatles after listening to their music. He didn't think they were going to go anywhere. He said they weren't good enough. I never let him live that down. Later on in life, I'd ask him, "What do you know about music? You turned down the Beatles." He usually laughed.

"Where is he from?" my father asked me the first time he met Dick. This was in my parent's house in Bonn. When I told him that Dick was from Kansas City, he said, "Is that where they just learned to walk upright?" That was his way of referring to someone who, in his opinion, lived in the middle of nowhere.

My father's sense of humor was acerbic. But it was also very rude. When Dick asked for my hand in marriage, he went to my dad on his own. I had no idea what he was doing. My mother and I were out shopping. What it was like in that room, I can't imagine. Dick hardly spoke a word of German, and my father spoke even less English. I'm sure it was as awkward as it was humorous. My father agreed to Dick's request, and my mother was very happy. However, Dick's mother wrote to his commanding officer and asked that he stop the marriage. I think she thought I was looking for a sponsor so that I could become an American citizen. Nevertheless, we were married in Frankfurt in 1962.

When I met Dick's family for the first time, his mother said to me, "Now you can become a citizen."

And I thought, "If she thinks that, then I will never become a citizen." And I kept this promise until 2013. By then, I think I had waited an appropriate amount of time.

CHAPTER 13

New York to Saigon

Dick left Germany before I did. As a G.I., he travelled on a troop transport back to New York. I followed shortly behind him. In the meantime, he was looking for work in the city. He felt some pressure in this. Recently released from the Army, his new bride was making her way to him, and without a job, our life together would be difficult indeed. I wasn't exactly planning on being dependent, but nevertheless if he could get a job by the time I arrived, things would be easier.

Before that could happen, I set sail for New York. I left on a large German passenger ship named the Bremen—after the port city where Helmut's side of the family moved after the war. My trip on that ship was about as romantic as any transatlantic voyage can be: It wasn't. I was sick much of the time. I also shared a room with someone. This wasn't such a bad thing, after all. She and I got to know each other on the voyage. She was also moving to New York City for the first time. So at least there was someone to talk with, and we had something in common.

Midway through the trip I received a telegram from my husband that set my mind at ease despite the seasickness. It read: "Just got a writer's job with ABC News. I am thrilled." And so was I to hear the news. It's a much happier way to come into a new country when you know that your husband is working.

Dick met me down at the docks. We had been apart by this point for several months and were very happy to be reunited. The pressure was also off him. He had gotten a job and not just any job, either. He was working as a writer for ABC News. This was exactly the kind of employment he was looking for. It's not easy to land a position at a prestigious company like that. But he had done it, and now we were together.

This was our new city and our new life. My first order of business was to get a job. Since I was working at Oppenheimer & Co. and their main offices were in New York, it might have been a good idea to see if I could get a transfer out of Frankfurt. But I was proud, and I didn't want to ask them for anything. I thought I could do it all on my own. In the back of my mind, I knew that if I failed to get a job in a reasonable amount of time then I could always fall back on them. But for the time being, it was all on me to get a job in the city.

Now I felt a similar pressure as my husband was under. I like a challenge. Until that point, my father had gotten me most of the jobs I had held. I preferred to do it on my own. I didn't need help from the company or anyone else.

I got results though, and was soon hired by a large broker as a research analyst. I liked this job because it allowed me to see inside a company and understand what was really going on.

My memories of New York beginning in 1965 are fond. I liked my job. I was living in a new and interesting place. New York was no Paris, but in the 1960s it seemed like the center of the world. And I had gotten there on my own.

One major memory remains of my time in the city. We were there for the blackout of 1965. Nearly the entire Northeast was out of power. I remember it because of Dick. As a young man he had been a volunteer firefighter. When the power went out that night, it was dark, and traffic immediately ground to a halt. Imagine Manhattan with no traffic lights. Everything stops, and people start getting angry quickly. Then horns start. My husband put on a long-sleeve white shirt, ran out into the intersection in front of our building, and began directing traffic as if this was something he did all the time. He looked official and was actually of help to the angry New Yorkers trapped in that dark gridlock.

But our time in the city was short. My husband was a journalist. And a good journalist can't remain in one place for long. Therefore, I knew what it meant when Dick said to me, "You can't get anywhere in your career without going to Vietnam." And he was right about that.

"That's fine with me," I said. "Why don't you propose that to ABC?"

He did. I didn't think he would get a response so quickly. It was only a short time before he told me he had been named Bureau Chief for ABC News, Saigon.

At the time I didn't even know the difference between Hanoi and Saigon. I soon noticed that a lot of Americans didn't know the difference, either. I told him I would go with him but that I would only stay with him in Saigon. Many of the wives would stay in Hong Kong, which was about 900 miles from Saigon, and they'd only get to see their husbands every ten weeks in the ten days off they had. I wanted no part of this. I didn't want to be separated from him for so long. And what was I going to do in Hong Kong, anyway? If he was going to live through a war so was I. The idea of staying in Manhattan was out of the question. My job, while fine, was also heading in a direction I didn't like. It's not what I envisioned doing in my future. The idea of traveling to a far-off country—and Vietnam, to me, could hardly have been farther off—was an adventure I wanted to have. There was no way I would sit in some Hong Kong hotel while Dick got to have all the fun.

I didn't consider the war. I knew the war was there; it's why we were going, after all. But I didn't even think for one moment about what the war was all about. Sitting at lunch one day with a friend who was also the wife of a journalist, I realized my carelessness with regard to this question. She asked, "What do you think about Vietnam? What do you think about our government and what they are doing there? Do you think they're right?"

And I remember saying, "I mean, they're your government. Why would they lie to you? I'm sure they have a good reason to be there. I'm sure it's okay." I guess I hadn't learned my lessons from World War II. I was too young. But as the war in Vietnam progressed, and I spent time there, I came to see the foolishness of the domino theory of Cold War foreign policy, but that did not make me pro-Communist. I had seen the Soviets up close, and I could not trust and would not tolerate a Stalinistic dictatorship.

As I spent more time "in country," I saw atrocities on both sides: American and Vietcong. I also know that American journalists largely refrained from covering Vietcong atrocities because if they did cover them, their stories often did not get any airtime back home. The American mind was turning against the war.

Yet in the summer of 1966, we were all still pretty naïve about what was going on. The predictions of victory for the Americans had been rosy, to say the least. In many ways, these predictions still rang true, but the facts on the ground were beginning to change the way people understood the war.

I was excited to get to Saigon. Getting off the plane, I was overwhelmed by the reality of the city. The air was bad. The city was congested and confusing. On the streets, the cars headed in every direction, and the cyclos would run you down. You could hardly cross the road on foot. But my impression right away was that this was a beautiful city. Saigon was once called the Pearl of the Orient, but sandbags and barbed wire kept that charm well-hidden. Many of the buildings had a French Colonial charm about them. In spite of the war, I took note of all this.

There was, of course, the problem of bombings. At the time, these bombings were the favorite pastime of the Vietcong. They would throw Molotov cocktails into any private businesses that catered to Westerners. I had not been aware of these before coming to Vietnam. But you became keenly aware anytime you sat in a restaurant. I learned quickly never to have my back to the door. On my first day in Saigon, an old hand told me always to watch the doors. So that was rule number one. It was like the Old West in that way. Sometimes if we sat at a table, we would all instinctively shuffle around our chairs to have a line of sight to the door. You could tell who was new when they didn't watch the doors.

We were staying in the Caravelle Hotel with the other journalists. CBS, ABC and the Australian Embassy were all located inside the hotel. Across the National Assembly Square from the Caravelle sat the Continental. The building exuded old French colonial charm. But it had no air conditioning. The writers preferred it probably because Graham Greene wrote *The Quiet American* right there on the terrace. But the TV people wanted modern amenities. That's why they lived in the Caravelle. NBC had an office across Tu Do Street in the old Eden Building. AP resided there also.

Together with the other Westerners we formed a group and became very close. You tend to grow together living under mutual threat. And there was a sense of imminent doom that's hard to understand outside of the situation. It felt like we were on the verge of an apocalypse. The war was tough. People got killed every day— civilians, soldiers, journalists—but Saigon was still a relatively safe city aside from the shelling, which often happened almost at random. Aside from this, we were safe and among friends in Saigon, but outside the gates Rome was burning.

Needless to say, we partied. It was not all fun and games, of course. People worked. I saw many journalists who really worked for their stories. I looked up to them, and through my husband I met many of them. But in Saigon the only thing you could do was socialize with other people like you. The Caravelle Hotel was like a hub for all kinds of Westerners who passed through on their tours of the area.

You often made friends for life under those circumstances. It was in Saigon that we met Martha and David. They had gotten married in '66, the same year David enlisted in the Navy and was made a Public Information Officer in Saigon. His entire family was in the Navy, and with the war on, it was something he could never have missed. This meant the newlyweds were separated, yet David and Martha were not the types to let things simply take their course if it wasn't the one they wanted.

When David noticed that all the other branches of the military had a newspaper, he proposed to whomever he served under in the Navy that they should also have a newspaper. They agreed, and since David had experience in the business through his family, he was allowed to run the operation.

At the same time, Martha was looking to move closer to Saigon so that she could see her husband more often. When she heard that an international school in Bangkok was hiring English teachers, Martha decided to apply. She got the job and quickly moved there. After that happened, David settled on a small printing firm in the city where he could get the newspaper printed. This printing and teaching arrangement allowed them to be together far more often than they otherwise would have been.

Dick met David in Saigon, and they became fast friends. Dick even helped the couple get a hotel room in the overbooked Caravelle for a weekend so they could be together. He did this by sending some journalists out into the field and using their room. Needless to say, Martha and David were very happy with that arrangement. We would continue our relationship until a tragedy split them apart, but that was much later on.

Our social life was always very interesting in Saigon. We celebrated Ted Koppel's birthday in February of 1967. We had several drinks, and Ted stood in the Nyguen Hue Street shouting, "You know, Dick, it's over when you're thirty. If you haven't made it by then, you're done." Ted was there, as was every other journalist, to make a name for himself. As to making it by 30, I think he might have been hasty with that assessment. It didn't hold true for him after all. But Ted was wonderful. He gave us some of our most memorable lines. He spoke with an Army Captain once. Beside the Captain was a young Lieutenant serving as the PAO officer. Whenever the Captain let off a string of swears or ugly assessments, the young officer would pipe up with an official version. He'd begin by saying, "What the Captain really means . . ." and then follow with his spiel. Ted told the story of the PAO officer, and "what the Captain really means" became a catch phrase for us for years.

Prior to the Tet Offensive there were very light moments, and we got to meet so many different people under what were strangely decadent circumstances. Teddy Kennedy came once to Vietnam and stayed at the Caravelle.

He sat like everybody else on the roof terrace where you could watch the spectacle of the war from a safe distance. Tracers looked like fireworks, and the deep rumbling of the B52 bombing sounded like thunder. Kennedy sat inside the restaurant writing notes, completely absorbed in reading over material and obviously trying to do his homework. The roof terrace made up half of the restaurant. At cocktail hour, everyone would come up there to watch the war. It was a spectacle. Even the Pan Am stewardesses would come up.

I thought of Ted as lazy playboy who had come for the photo op. It turned out he really cared. Seeing him in that restaurant, looking out over the city and doing work, changed my mind about him. I told him about this years later when I covered him running for President. I told him how I came to respect him then.

The war was out there. We all knew it. And Teddy was attempting to understand what was really going on. Here was a U.S. Senator, sitting in the rooftop lounge of a five-star hotel, looking out over a war. He could make all the observations he wanted, but the war was a reality.

Tet would change everything. Before fighting reached the Cholon suburb of Saigon, my husband, as ABC's Bureau Chief, invited all media in town to the Eskimo Restaurant. David often came with us there. The Eskimo was a Chinese restaurant in Cholon which we completely took over on Sunday nights. The owner watched out for our safety, and the food was great. This was "our" restaurant. Their Korean winter kimchi was something you had to be careful of, though.

On one occasion, the actor and Navy reservist Glenn Ford came to Vietnam on a VIP tour. We took him out to that little restaurant. Since he was in the Reserves, he had to take tours of active duty. I also think he had just come off an affair with Rita Hayworth, his neighbor, and was escaping to Vietnam to lay low for a while. Anyway, he came out, and my husband threw a party at our little Chinese restaurant in Cholon.

Glenn reached out for the Korean winter kimchi and I told him: "You have to be very careful of that. They keep it in the ground longer. It is much hotter. Don't chew it on your tongue; chew it on the side of your mouth."

"Oh, I'm used to Asian food from when we shot the *Little Tea House*," which was a movie he had filmed a few years prior. When he said that, I knew that he was thinking of Japanese food, and this Korean winter kimchi was something else entirely. But he didn't listen to me. He was sorry immediately. He turned bright red. His mouth was burning and his eyes were watering. I wanted to say, "I told you so."

Later, our party spilled out into the streets, but we had no ride back to the hotel. There was a van coming for us, but it would not arrive until much later. Glenn wanted to leave right away. He looked around from the curb, and there was a military bus coming. This bus was for soldiers and was going in another direction entirely. When

Glenn saw the bus, he jumped into action. He flagged the driver down. Glenn at that time was a Lieutenant Colonel in the Reserves.

We stood outside the door in a group, some with drinks in hand, as Glenn told the driver that we all needed a ride. The driver told him that he couldn't give us a ride because the Caravelle was nowhere near his route. Glenn was a famous Hollywood actor, but as a Lieutenant Colonel he also outranked this poor Army driver. The driver probably knew his face, too.

Glenn pulled rank and got the poor driver to take our group of unruly civilians and a few officers back to the Caravelle Hotel. We were partying on the bus. It was as if we took the Eskimo with us as we drove across town, minus the kimchi. No one seemed to mind there was a war on. There were a few servicemen on the bus who missed their stops, but they didn't complain. It was very much like some buddy movie—a war comedy where the G.I.s go out and do something crazy while on leave. But this wasn't the real thing for Glenn. The G.I.s fighting the war knew the real thing. And it was coming home to everyone very soon.

CHAPTER 14

War Correspondent

I was living as Mrs. Richard Rosenbaum in Saigon. This fact did not make me happy. I wanted to do more. I had come here under the auspice of "wife," but I was not cut out to be just the wife of someone. I immediately began volunteering at the Third Field Hospital in Saigon. This at least gave me something more valuable to do. I found out quickly that I could really be of use to the wounded and sick men.

Soldiers were sick all the time in Vietnam. They suffered from encephalitis or malaria, or they were shot or hit with shrapnel. Any number of injuries sent them to the hospital. But life there was often hard and boring. There's nothing worse for a soldier than boredom. Poker was big with these guys, so I started to play to keep them company and have something for them to do. They looked forward to when I came. They had been cooped up for so long, both in the hospital and among soldiers, that just playing poker with a female civilian became an important part of their days. I would "doll" myself up for them. They liked it. I often went to the hospital three times a week. It was rewarding. I also got good at poker. After a few months of my visits, one of the G.I.s said, "There she is. Hide your money." And I thought, "Damn right!"

I was very good at poker, but Scrabble was another story. I learned English in Great Britain, and now that I was among Americans, I was still catching on to American English. Of course I was a non-native English speaker, and these guys knew that. I swear they would make up words. A couple of the guys would always throw out these ten-letter words full of Qs and Zs. I called them on it whenever it happened.

"No, that's not a word. You are cheating, taking advantage of a German. I challenge that word," I shouted.

"I thought we had a lady here."

"This lady wants a dictionary."

As much fun as I had working in the hospital I was still looking for more. The first few months of my stay in Saigon were relatively quiet compared to what would come later on, but that didn't mean they weren't interesting.

My friends were journalists. Together we liked to go to the tailor and have what we called the "perfect correspondent" suits made. These were like safari jackets with lots of pockets for notebooks, pencils, and stuff like that, and probably joints for a lot of them. I had several of these made in the colors they offered, which were darker blue, black, and beige. We wore them because they were comfortable. If you wore a dress in that climate, you were soaked in sweat after half an hour.

In the first two or three months, we spent our time just getting acclimated, and because Dick was not yet Bureau Chief, we had to switch rooms every week. He started out as assistant until the man who was in that position had filled him in on the job. Two months later, Dick became Chief. In the meantime, we had to take whatever rooms we could get. When he finally became Bureau Chief, we got our own room. There was a shortage of rooms for reporters. This meant that you moved from open room to open room. You shared your room with anyone who was not in town, either out of country or in the field. The hotels were filled, with up to six people holding claim to one room. We didn't all sleep there at the same time, but wherever an empty room opened up, that's where you would stick people. Each network had an allotment, and you had to make do with that. With people coming in and out of town all the time, it could get complicated.

About the time that Dick and I settled into the Bureau Chief's suite, something happened that changed everything. I knew the correspondent for the German Press Agency. There were not many Germans in Vietnam, and we all knew one another. The correspondent had to leave for a few weeks. Before he left he said, "Could you fill in for me?" I was walking across the National Assembly Square with Dick to go to the "Five O'clock Follies" when he approached me. I would often go to these press briefings with my husband.

Becoming a reporter of the German Press Agency meant that I would have to file two stories a day. I had never written a news piece in my life. My husband accepted for me right away. "Sure, she can," he said.

"I guess. Sure, I can."

The correspondent and Dick taught me the essentials of journalism, which they described as "who, what, where, when, why and how." Apparently this was all I needed to know. They assured me it was very easy. Of course I had written before in Germany for a financial newsletter, so I was familiar with writing. However, I didn't bother to tell them how I much I knew. I simply listened as they both were worthy teachers.

"You just have to go to the Five O'Clock Follies everyday and write two stories," my husband told me. The follies were the daily military briefings, where the official version of the day's events was given. Of course, the official version was not always what happened, and in many cases, the assessment was much different than the truth. So reporting straight from the follies was not the most in-depth form of journalism I could have been practicing. I knew this going in. After all, I had been around journalists since coming to Saigon and also before, while we lived in New York. I knew what kind of news came out of these press briefings. Nevertheless, I had to learn how to do it one way or another. The best way was to jump in and do it. The follies gave me that opportunity.

But reporting from the follies and the official version of things was boring. I knew right away that if I was going to write an interesting story, I actually had to go out and see something worth writing about. My first story proved this to me. It came from our pool correspondent's firsthand account. We learned through the follies that the aircraft carrier USS Forrestal was on fire. The military offered to fly in a reporter to cover the event. We chose Johnny Apple of *The New York Times*.

One of the Forrestal's fighter aircrafts had, due to an electrical shortage, fired one of its rockets. This rocket struck the fuel tank on the deck of another aircraft, which in turn caused a massive fire that killed almost the entire firefighting crew sent to extinguish the blaze.

Senator John McCain was in one of the planes that caught fire. He escaped just before his plane exploded.

The incident was terrible, as the fire caused a chain reaction on the deck, engulfing the planes and igniting their payloads. The men worked to push some of the planes off the deck to ensure the fire would spread no further.

Later that night, Apple came back to the Rex Hotel where the follies were held. The Americans commandeered the hotel and billeted troops there. We were all familiar with the hotel outside of the follies because on Sundays we all went to its rooftop restaurant. The food was okay, but beside the cash register sat a large bottle of malaria pills like breath mints. This made it easy for everyone to take their weekly medicine.

What sticks out most clearly in my mind was Johnny Apple's retelling of the story to the group assembled at the Rex. He was so good. He walked into the room of reporters. We were silent. This wasn't some military careerist; this was Johnny Apple. He talked a good picture. So good, that I saw every moment. He spoke of the heroism and adrenaline of the men fighting to keep the whole ship from burning; of the holes in the deck spilling jet fuel into the crew quarters; of the first firefighters battling until there were only a few survivors left; of pilots in burning planes who hit the deck and ran for their lives, or jumped off into the man-overboard net to escape incineration; and of the seamen and Marines who finally contained the blaze.

Here was a story, and here was a storyteller, and that's who I wanted to be. I faithfully recorded every quote and retold the story as he had told it to the pool, so that my readers could get the same sense as me. I didn't have a clear picture of whom my readers were at this point, as I had never written a story for a large audience. I didn't even know if this style of story would be accepted. I can't say that I didn't care, but I wanted to tell the story the right way.

I wrote in the first person. I wrote as it happened. This was the type of reporting I preferred to read: writers like George Plimpton. And damn it, this was the type of writing I was going to do. Why should I be boring? There were plenty of boring writers. I didn't think the world needed another one. I was slightly apprehensive about what the result would be. The way I was writing was a drastic departure from the way newswire stories were traditionally written, especially in Germany.

But my story was immediately met with praise back home in Germany. The correspondent whose job I was covering was not happy with my style of writing. Actually, he was happy with my writing, but he was not happy that I was able to get away with writing like that.

"Thea, if I wrote like that they would fire me, but you get away with it."

It wasn't long before he gave the job over to me entirely. He was the South East Asian correspondent and preferred not to be in Vietnam if he could help it. I became his reporter. He was happy to have me there. For him, it was easier. He lived in Hong Kong, and that meant he didn't have to go to Vietnam as much any more. And he did mostly political stories.

I loved the idea of being a journalist and of writing how I felt I should write. Since the time when I wrote stories of Africa, I had always envisioned myself as a writer. But I had imagined that I was too stupid to do it. No matter what I did in my life, I had this nagging sense of inferiority, and so to come out and actually try to become a journalist was out of the question for me. That's exactly what I was now, and I was going to do a good job of it.

As I began to venture beyond the bounds of the Five O'Clock Follies, my life became a little more interesting. I was not a homebody before that point, but I also wasn't going out and nearly getting killed. My husband supported me all the way, although I know that sometimes, especially later on, I could make him nervous. But the only caution he ever gave me was to always go with someone else. He didn't want me to be alone.

But this was all in advance of Tet, when the war really changed. Tet was the point where the American public truly turned against the war, and it was the point for me where I really saw what war was. Before that, I took risks for stories, but the risk wasn't real to me in the way it was after Tet and Hue.

One of the stories I did during that time involved taking a flight up to the mountains with the Air Force to Pleiku. I was there to see the 633d Combat Support Group. These guys flew interdictions, special ops and rescue missions close to the Cambodian border along the Ho Chi Min trail. They were known for close air support where they flew in Sky Raider light bombers. When I was under attack in Nam O, it could have been a Sky Raider that hit the other side of the street. That was close air support, for sure.

These pilots took a lot of action. They were also very brave, and they knew it. They had a real flyboy mentality: they were arrogant and loved girls, partying, and making fun. What better group to do a story on? It was also my intention to go on a bombing run and report on that, but first we had to sit around and wait. This was always the case during the war. There was action, then nothing. "Hurry up and wait" was our watchword. It became a running joke, and because of the downtime both journalists and G.I.s had, we often played poker. I had learned to play in my time at the Third Field Hospital. Now at Pleiku, there was a group of flyboys sitting around a table and playing.

"Do you mind if I play? I'm bored," I asked.

"Do you know how?" one of them said.

"A little bit." I never let on that I could play, so they thought I was an easy target. I was really very good. We began to play, and I started to win and take their money. One of the guys got a little upset.

"You said you didn't know how to play. A lady wouldn't do that."

"Sorry about that, guys. I guess I'm not a lady."

I heard that a lot during the war. Especially during poker whenever I started to win, one of the guys almost always said something to the effect that I wasn't a lady. It was all fun to me, although some of these guys might have wanted to make me pay for it later on. In fact, I think that's exactly what they tried to do. That was fine—I could anticipate that—but what I hadn't anticipated were the Montagnards. Indigenous to Vietnam, they were at war with the Vietnamese, but they supposedly loved Americans.

While we were at the airbase, someone suggested we visit these people in their village in the mountains. "We can take a drive," they said. Driving off base in the jungle wasn't my idea of a good time. I asked about the Vietcong. "The Vietcong won't go anywhere near the Montagnards. Those people are ruthless."

I thought that this would be a good diversion and that I would get to report on an aspect of Vietnam about which not many people knew. So we packed into Jeeps. A colleague, the flyboys and I drove over to the Montagnard village from the American air base at Pleiku. We traveled through jungle mountain roads. The VC could have hidden at any corner, but they really didn't go near the Montagnards.

When we arrived, they were having a celebration. The village consisted of a series of small huts in the highlands. Just alongside the village we passed a little cemetery, where I saw a few people standing. I noticed all these huge vases, which turned out to be full of rice wine.

While the villagers were very nice to us, the flyboys were another story. One or two of them sat at the poker table with me, and they remembered. These guys were always trying to make fun of me because I was a woman. They thought they could get the better of me. One of the guys started saying, "You have to drink the rice wine. It's a custom here. Otherwise, you'll really offend them."

At first I was skeptical. I looked into the keg of rice wine the Montagnards had made. The wine fermented in the barrels between layers of rice cakes. The Air Force guy spoke up again. "You have to drink three layers of wine. That's the way it is. You take the straw and hang it in the keg. Three layers," he reiterated. Since there was a narrow neck on top, they put a piece of straw or twig down into the wine, and you had to drink until you exposed the end of the straw. They considered that one layer. After that, they added more water and shook it up to mix the alcohol, and you drank again. They wanted me to drink three layers of this.

"You have to do it."

It was their monthly death ceremony, and they were having a celebration. Part of it was in honor of their dead, and when they finished drinking they danced around the graves. The villagers waved to us that we had to do it, too. They insisted we become part of their ceremony.

I participated under this pressure. I took the straw from a Montagnard's hand. He smiled as I leaned down to drink my three layers. The flyboys all cheered behind me. It was obvious that they had done this before. I couldn't tell how much they were messing with me and how much was true, but it did seem true that this was a ceremony for the Montagnard dead.

I drank my layer. The wine tasted awful. A little Montagnard man leaned in and poured the water back to the same level. I noticed that he didn't really shake up the wine, so the second layer wasn't as alcoholic as the first, and neither was the third. I think he was being nice to me. He secretly didn't want me to get sick, but he appreciated that I was honoring their custom.

When I pulled away from the vase, one of the pilots said, "You are lucky. If you came up another day, you would have had to drink buffalo blood."

"Thank God for small favors," I said.

Then I looked around. I saw that when they finished a jar of wine, which the pilots did frequently, they threw the rice cake from the bottom of the vase on the ground. The pigs and dogs were eating these cakes and were drunk, running back and forth in the silliest way around the village. Some of the animals were stone drunk. I had been living in Saigon with journalists long enough, so I was no stranger to drinking, but this wine was tough to take.

I felt a bit nauseous after drinking all that wine. For the life of me, I wouldn't throw up. These guys probably had a bet about that, and I wouldn't give them the satisfaction. But before I had any chance to dwell on the state of my stomach, a villager said I had to dance with them to honor their dead. By this point, I was feeling the effects of the alcohol rather than just its taste, and I was doing all right. I went with them into the graveyard, and we danced around the graves of their ancestors, all of us in varying states of drunkenness. We danced what was like a Watusi. There were advisors and pilots from the Air Force dancing around in circles with the Montagnards and a handful of journalists. We danced and drank far into the night, and later I slept in a room with everyone else.

The next morning I flew out on a Sky Raider for a bombing run. The planes had three bombs on each side. I was really hung-over. I think the pilot was, too. He laughed when I got into the seat beside him on the runway in the morning. It was just a two-seater. As we took off he told me with a grin like a little boy's on his face, "I got shot down three weeks ago."

"Oh, that's great."

"It's no problem. They got me out. We have a survival kit right here," he pointed. "We have these appetite suppressants. You take these with a little water, and you're not hungry. You'll be all right."

I'm thinking that these guys really want to mess with me. Now he's just having fun. Finally, we reach our target. I knew of the heavy bombing that happened in Germany. But this is dive-bombing. He acquires his target then takes his little plane straight down with me in it. My stomach is in my mouth. It made any roller coaster feel tame. And once again I'm trying not to vomit. "Oh, God, don't let me throw up all over this guy's plane." When we reach the limit of our dive, the bomb comes off. He pulls up, flattens out and heads back up again. Now he's turning. He finds the next target and back into the dive we go. There's a moment at the top and bottom of the dive where I feel weightless. When we dive, it feels like we are falling from the sky. When we ascend, it feels like we are shot from a cannon. I only catch glimpses of the explosions when we double-back to drop more bombs. But we are away from our target long before the bombs hit the ground.

I'm counting the number of dives we take. I can't wait until this is over—the sooner the better. We hit the fifth dive then go back up and around, then take the sixth dive. I'm thanking the bombing gods in my head for ending this thing, but then we drop again. Maybe my count was wrong. It could have been under the circumstances. We dive an eighth time, and again and again. This isn't right.

"Hey, how many times are we going to dive? Shouldn't we be done?"

"No," he said, "We're not done. We have a hanging bomb."

"Why didn't you tell me we had a hanging bomb? On whose side is it?"

"Your side."

"What does that mean?" I ask.

"It means we can't get rid of the bomb."

"Tell me in reality what that means?"

"Well, in reality, it means we can't land. Or we could land, but we'd probably blow up. We've got to get rid of it."

He was really making my day now. First they got me so drunk that I nearly threw up, and now this. "Can't we land and just parachute out?"

"No, we can't land and just parachute out."

"What can we do?"

"We have to try to get it off. It's on your side. Reach in that panel, there." And then he told me what I was looking for. I couldn't even say what he had me doing. I was feeling around blindly for a cable or something. I started pulling to release the bomb. At that point, I was so sick I didn't care anymore what happened to the plane or what

I pulled. He was telling me to pull. This was just a tiny little plane. I grabbed a hook inside the wing and began pulling. Then the bomb let go and dropped down onto the countryside.

We were happy. But only God knows where it landed or whom it may have hit.

"You know," he said, "I really admire you. You didn't throw up all over my plane. You hung in there. So I'll fly you all the way back to Saigon."

"That's good," I said, "Because I have a party to go to."

"I'll even let you fly the plane."

But I turned him down on that one. We returned to Saigon. He said goodbye and that he hoped my party went well. I got off his plane. I told him I would never forget that flight. He smiled, and that was the last I saw of that pilot.

I got ready for the party. If I remember correctly, it was a diplomatic party. I told the story of my time with the Montagnards and the Air Force guys to a group of journalists over cocktails. "You had to drink the rice wine, too!" was the response I got.

This was still before the Tet offensive. It wasn't long after that that I had cause to be offended and driven even further. Of course, we had parties like these all the time at the Caravelle Hotel and around town. Westerners were always throwing parties. It's how we coped. The group there was very small, so all the same people came to the parties.

One night Hubert Humphrey came to town. He was running for President. He was another of the VIPs. He was there for the inauguration of President Thieu and Vice President Ky. The party was at the Presidential Palace, but from its title you shouldn't get the idea that it was all splendor and opulence. The Palace was just a large, plain hall. The entrance was fairly small and in a corner. Humphrey was standing outside in the foyer, talking to people at the door, when mortars hit. Mortar fire is very distinct; it sounds a certain way. Three mortar rounds hit. One was right in the garden of the Palace. A lot of people hit the ground. The Secret Service was on top of Humphrey in a second, although I didn't see him actually go down since my view was blocked. I didn't hit the ground, either. I ran toward Humphrey, who dusted himself off. He was looking at me, so I asked him, "What do you think about this hello from Saigon?"

Humphrey replied, "We're not getting scared off that easily. But hopefully that's it for the welcome." Then the party continued. Later, a reporter for the *Saigon Post* wanted to know what I had said to Humphrey and what he answered. There were also other correspondents who immediately asked what he said. I gave them the quote. I was very happy to be interviewed. But when the morning's paper came out, I was shocked to find that I was quoted as Mrs. Richard Rosenbaum when I told them my name was Thea Rosenbaum of the DPA. Even then, they still had my name wrong.

It really pissed me off. I didn't like it. And I thought, "I want to do something about this."

I decided I needed to get out of town and into the field. I signed up for every press junket I could find with Military Assistant Command Vietnam (MACV for short). We called it Macvie. We could get in touch with them from the Rex Hotel. They ran trips to areas deemed interesting by the military, like the USS Forrestal. But with them you often got as much of the truth as from the Five O'Clock Follies. The scenes you were shown had usually ended hours or days beforehand. But if you wanted to get out into the field—and I did—this was the fastest way to do it.

I would get better at getting into the field on my own with time, but for now I had to rely on MACV. On an occasion later on, I was taken by helicopter somewhere outside of Saigon in the Iron Triangle. The Americans had developed a near obsession with body counts. And I guess since the press questioned their figures, the military sought to prove what they said. I went along by helicopter to a field. There had been an engagement the night before. The military gave figures of how many they had killed. Sure enough, they had stacked bodies like cordwood in the field to make it easier to count.

"They're all there, if you want to count them," a glib PIO (Press Information Officer) said.

"No, thank you. That won't be necessary."

That was later on, but for my first trip with them I had to try for several days before I could get in on a press junket. It was my first time, after all, and there was limited space. When I finally did connect with a press junket, we flew out on a military helicopter headed for an old rubber plantation near the Cambodian border, near a city called Anh Loc. On board with me was a crew from ABC News.

The Americans believed that they were near the end of the Ho Chi Minh Trail, which is why they paid the area so much attention. The fighting had been heavy over the last week, and they had just had some engagements the night prior. The military was eager to show off their accomplishments, which would probably have included a stack of bodies.

You could see the plantation laid out in an old French colonial design as we flew in. In a way, it was like an American plantation with a large white house overlooking it all. Once full of rubber trees, there were no more trees. They all must have been defoliated in an attempt to find out where the NVA and VC were hiding. The Americans believed there was a base somewhere near there, but they couldn't find it. At that point, they didn't know about the tunnels spider-webbing the area.

We landed. The PAO (Public Affairs Officer) came over, eager to show us around. Near our position there was a heavy entrenchment of artillery. He motioned in that direction. I was new to this whole enterprise, and I had something else on my mind.

"Where is your ladies' room?"

A young G.I. pointed to a bush on the other side of the plantation. "You see those bushes? Right one's the ladies' latrine. Left bush is the men's latrine."

I nodded to him and walked over and did my business. When I returned from the right bush, I thought, "I can cut straight through the field." I started to walk across the old plantation. Choppers were coming into the landing zone behind us. I couldn't hear a thing. But I saw people waving at me. It was the G.I. who had sent me to the latrine. I couldn't tell what he was saying, so I was waiving back happily as if everything was fine. Then the rotors died down and the G.I. yelled, "Minefield!"

I wish he would have told me before I went to the bushes that if I veered off into the field I would be in a minefield. You'd think that was an important piece of information to tell someone. When I heard him, I stopped dead, turned around and began retracing my steps back to the bushes so I could walk out the way I came in. When I came back to the position where the artillery was placed, a young lieutenant greeted my return by saying, "This is no place for a lady."

"I guess not," I said, "But it's a place for me." After that, he gave me a briefing. Then I said, "I could do with a cold Coca-Cola." I was kidding, but the G.I. started digging in the ground. Sure enough, he had a Coke there. It was still pretty cool. I couldn't believe that he could come up with a cold Coke in the middle of the jungle.

"Next thing you're going to tell me is that we'll have deliveries of turkeys at Thanksgiving."

"Probably will," he replied.

That wasn't the only time I had been told something along the lines, "This is no place for a lady." Every once in a while in a dicey situation, somebody would say the same thing. I seemed to hear it most often among lobbyists or arms dealers in Saigon. They were there to sell whatever it was they sold, like the rep for the M16. They had already sold them to the military, but they were still trying to sell them to the public. The best way to do that was through journalists. Very often people like that would say it to me. I always ignored them, but I heard it so often that I remembered the phrase. My husband and I often would joke that if I ever wrote a book I would have to call it *No Place for a Lady*. Dick even had a blank notebook bound in leather for me. The spine read: *No Place for a Lady*. At some point, I was asked by a German publisher to write a book, but he wanted me to turn it into a novel so that I could add invented sex scenes. I declined. If I was going to write my book, it would be *my* book, and not some trumped-up novel.

CHAPTER 15

Airborne School

I took every interesting assignment I could get my hands on. I heard that reporters were doing Airborne training with the South Vietnamese based outside of Tan Son Nhat airport in Saigon. I hate to say that everything happened at a cocktail party in Saigon, but I was talking with a friend at a cocktail party when we heard about this possibility.

"I'm going to do that," I said.

The woman I was talking with thought I was joking at first. But I wasn't. I said, "No. I'm going to do the Airborne training." It sounded like a great story to me. If I was ever going to be more than just the wife of somebody, I was going to have to do this.

This was around Christmas of 1967. Until this point, I heard stories of the South Vietnamese Airborne troops. They were said to be very good, very brave, and they had a high success rate against the Vietcong. I knew that the best way to report on them was to become one of them. At least I could get really close. My mind was made up.

I wrote a letter to General Westmorland asking his permission to take the training. I also wrote to General Vien, Joint Chief of Staff for the South Vietnamese Army. Within three days I got the okay. It was very quick. I was ready. Training began immediately. Right about that time, Dick had resolved to get our friends Martha and David a room together at the Caravelle Hotel. I don't know whether Dick had offered to do it, or if David had asked. But as Bureau Chief, Dick had the power to put people, typically journalists and the like, up in different rooms. He also could send people out into the field on assignment. The Caravelle was notoriously overbooked. There was never an open room, and people mostly shared time in rooms as they came in and out of the field. This arrangement made for interesting juggling. So when Martha flew in from Bangkok for several days, Dick arranged to have two correspondents sent out into the field to make room for the couple. They were very happy to have the room for a few days. We saw them often during this period. We even went out to the Eskimo together one night.

The day to begin my Airborne training came, and I drove my VW Beetle the thirty minutes from the Caravelle Hotel to Tan Son Nhat Airport where the South Vietnamese Airborne Headquarters was. Traffic was light that morning. The airport was on a dusty stretch of land broken up here and there by patches of trees. Tan Son Nhat itself was huge. The commercial airport part of it only comprised a small section. The rest of the land was shared by the American Air Force base and the South Vietnamese Airborne; MACV was there as well.

I parked in the lot and walked over to the base. I was wearing a military press pass, so I was allowed to enter. I met Colin Leinster, the photographer from *Life Magazine*, at the gate. He was training for the same reasons I was, so we walked in together. It was around seven o'clock in the morning. We entered a plain, large warehouse-type structure. An American military advisor greeted us inside.

He introduced me to my trainer Sergeant Song. I don't know what I expected, but they were both very nice. I suppose they had to be. Then the sergeant handed us both a pair of leather airborne boots and steel helmets to wear.

"Jungle boots are not strong enough in the ankles," he said, but didn't bother to describe the helmet's advantage. I guess it was self-explanatory.

The sergeant accompanied us to the training area. The grounds consisted of a mock airplane, a smaller nine-foot tower, and the feared 34-foot tower. It looked like any old military training site. There was also plenty of room to run, which they weren't afraid to make us do.

We joined the class that was underway. The introduction was brief, then we just filed into line with the other troops. When they told us to run, we ran. When they told us to jump, we jumped. To me it was like boot camp. I was exhausted, and I know Colin was, too. The first day we had to run several miles. They also taught us how to fall the "right way" in anticipation of our first jump. The jumps would be the culmination of our training. We had to do several, six in all; at least one of the jumps had to be out of a helicopter. The idea of jumping from the helicopter frightened me. I put that out of my mind for the moment.

Later we were taken and shown the parachutes we'd have to become familiar with. That day's training ended at around 4:00 p.m. I was happy to head home. I walked across the airport to where I had parked my VW and returned to the Caravelle. When I got home, I didn't know whether I should fall down dead, give up, or start crying, I was so exhausted. I thought of quitting, but my pride won out. There was no way I would quit.

The next morning, as per orders, I arrived at 6:00 a.m. It was more of the same. They drilled into us different aspects of jumping and what could possibly happen to our parachutes as we descended. One of the worst problems the trainers described was a "Mae West." This is named after the busty Hollywood actress. It meant that sometimes a cord could get tangled over the top of your chute. This gives it a heart shape or the shape of a brassiere, hence the name. Despite the silliness of the name, if you got one of these, you were in trouble. To get out of the Mae West you had to pull the line for your backup parachute.

We also learned how to look to the windsocks for guidance, what they meant, and how we should adjust our canopy accordingly. If the wind came from this direction, you pulled the cord on the right when you were on the ground so that it wouldn't catch the wind and drag you, and so forth. It would have been simple if the consequences weren't so dire. I was a little apprehensive about jumping.

I wouldn't get that chance for a while. It was only my third or fourth day. We were on the nine-foot tower, learning how to land from our fall. I was already covered in bruises and scratches. But the nine-foot tower would prove tougher than the 34-foot tower.

For the training, you had to stand up on top of the structure. Then a trap door released and there was only half a second to align yourself and land properly. That was about a half a second too fast for me. I skipped landing with my feet and hit the ground with the side of my ass instead. I tell you, it hurt. I shouted when I hit the ground and tried to stand up. I was immediately limping. The trainer who was there saw what happened. I was in a great deal of pain. They excused me for the day because I could hardly walk.

I couldn't just go home. Later on, I was slated to volunteer my time at the Third Field Hospital in Saigon. I slid into my VW as carefully as possible. Every bump on those well-worn roads hurt. When I arrived for duty at the hospital, I was in rough shape.

"What's wrong with you?" a doctor friend asked.

"I fell off the nine-foot tower onto my ass."

He smiled a little and said, "Well, step into my office." He motioned to the door, and I followed him. Inside he said, "Now drop your pants."

"No way, I'm not dropping my pants. You get your kicks looking at a blue ass."

"Come on, I'm a doctor."

"Yeah, come on. You get a hard-on just looking at a girl's behind, don't you?"

He finally convinced me that he had to see it. How else was he going to know what was wrong with me if he couldn't look? So I pulled down one side of my pants. I kept my eye on him, and he started laughing and laughing. He thought it was the funniest thing. "That looks like a nice plum."

"This is exactly why I didn't want to show you."

But then he became serious and told me there was no way I was going back to training for at least three weeks. I took his word for it. Before too long I was back on the course and doing the training. I was determined to take the five jumps, graduate, and get the wings they awarded. I had gone this far already.

In the meantime, Colin had moved on and taken his first jump. It didn't go so well. When he jumped, he got a Mae West in his chute. When he tried to pull his backup chute, it failed to deploy fully. In that case, he had what they called in training a "streamer." This was another humorously phrased term, which in reality was deadly. The military was always good for such things. So since his backup would not deploy, and his main chute was not fully open because of the Mae West, he came to the ground much faster than he should have. He really hurt his back.

Some of my friends tried to dissuade me from continuing the training after that. They explained that I had already proven that I would do it, and that I didn't have any more to prove. They didn't know me very well if they thought I would leave something I started unfinished.

I returned to training as soon as I was able. And this was under the three weeks the doctor had recommended. I had to go through the day's grind again. This time, they took me up on the 34-foot tower, where you were buckled into a harness and attached to a steel cable that took you at a high speed across the grounds for several hundred yards. After doing this, I felt that nothing could touch me.

There was nothing I could do after that but prepare for my first jump. I was ready. I knew I would do it. When the day came, I marched into the airplane with the rest of the troops. It was a small aircraft, and we stayed low. They connected the cord for my parachute to a carabineer that attached to a cable in the aircraft, just as we had practiced. This ensured your chute pulled open automatically when you jumped from the plane.

They put me second in line to go out the door. Now I would have to go, no matter what happened. I was afraid. The men in the plane knew I was afraid and started laughing at me. But then they began singing their military songs. This cheered me up.

As we got ready to jump I thought, "Well, there's no way back." They weren't going to unclip me. That was for sure.

The sight master was ready at the door. The wind blew in my face. I just focused on this man. Then he screamed, "GO!" The first parachutist went. Then "GO!" and I stepped out of the plane. I didn't even think about it. I just went as I was told. The cable I was connected to released my chute immediately and I was floating down with the other soldiers. From up above it almost seemed there wasn't a war happening at all. It all seemed so peaceful. Though I did imagine what it would be like to actually have to jump into a war zone. I got a sighting on the Landing Zone and the windsocks, and I was all ready to land.

We all landed safely, but my test wasn't over. Sergeant Song was on the ground waiting for me. "You can go make second jump. You go. Chopper coming right now," he said.

"Yes, but not today," I replied.

"Yes, today."

"No, Song, I can't do it. My legs are still soft."

This had not been on the itinerary. I really tried to get out of it. I didn't want to jump from the chopper at all and especially without any warning. When I did that, he told me that he would be fired if I didn't do it. "I will be in trouble. Very important person flying the chopper. General Vien piloting the chopper." This man was Joint Chief of Staff for the South Vietnamese Army. His position just increased the pressure on me, and Song shamed me into it. I agreed. Sergeant Song smiled and walked me over to the helicopter. It was ready and waiting to go. The rotors were already spinning. Inside, the sergeant handed me another parachute. I prepared myself. I couldn't believe I was going to have to do this twice in one day. And I had been afraid at the idea of the helicopter jump from the very beginning.

When we got off the ground, they flew somewhat lower than the airplane had. I was worried about the tail rotor. I just kept imagining that I would jump out and be chopped to pieces by it.

Song yelled to me to get ready. I put my feet outside the chopper and they were immediately pulled to the back by the wind. I thought they were going to be hit by the rotor. Of course it was on the other side. That's why you sit on the right side, not on the left. But what did I know? I was panicking, and I had never trained for this. He shouted, "Jump!" But I didn't jump. I climbed back inside the helicopter. I could see that he was just devastated I didn't do it. That's when the pilot, General Vien, turned around and said: "Ahh, don't worry. You can do it. I will turn around. You go again. You jump."

I looked at Song. "I can't do this. You're going to have to push me out really hard so I fall far away from the chopper." And they did. We flew back to the place where I was supposed to jump. Then Song pushed me really hard from the chopper. I tumbled as I went. The chute opened and I headed to the ground. Immediately I had a twister, but I did as I was trained and it came loose. I only had 5,000 feet to fall. Down below, they had removed the windsocks. I think they thought everyone was done landing. Now I had no idea where the wind was coming from. As I fell I kept licking my fingers to get them wet so that I could judge which way the wind was blowing. But I had no idea. I thought it was coming from all sides.

When I landed, the wind was up. I hit the ground without trouble, but the wind pulled my chute and me with it along the ground. I was so weak by that point that I couldn't stop it. I heard someone shouting, "Minefield."

"Not again."

Then a group of little children ran out into the field and knocked my chute down so it wasn't picking up wind anymore.

Later, when they landed the helicopter, Sergeant Song asked me, "Why were you going to land in the minefield?"

"Did I know that was a minefield?"

"Oh, I thought I told you. Anyway, we'll go back." Then he started hugging and kissing me, and he got very lovey-dovey. "Let's go back to the training base," he said.

I didn't know why we were going. Then he said, "We have to go up on top of the 34-foot tower." I followed him. Under the tower there were a hundred or so South Vietnamese soldiers having a midday break. It was very hot.

I followed him to the top of the tower. I couldn't see why he needed me to be up there. Then he grabbed me and hugged me. He was just a little Cambodian man, but he was very strong. His attempt was just short of an attack. He was trying to seduce me strongly. "Oh, you shithead," I thought.

Then I said, "There are all these soldiers down there, what are you doing?" But I didn't yell. I was worried about yelling for help because I was afraid that if the men below knew what was happening they might want to join in. I desperately wanted him to stop. He soon got the picture that I wasn't going in for this sort of thing. He let me go. He had gotten my pants partway off, and I pulled them back on. We got down off the tower and I said, "We're not going to have to do this with every jump, are we?"

Afterward, I purposely took Sergeant Song to the Caravelle Hotel to meet my husband. The Sergeant looked ashamed, as he should have.

In front of a bunker in Khe Sanh

I hit the ground in Nam-O, TET Offensive 1968

Interview with presidential candidate Jimmy Carter
in his back yard in Plains, Georgia

Having fun with the stewardesses on the Press Plane

Being changed into a clown

Greeting President Reagan, who is entering a room to be interviewed

After an Interview in Washington D.C. with President G. Bush

The whole team in Germany after an interview with M. Gorbachev

Muhammad Ali is talking to the press before a fight in Las Vegas

My retirement party in Washington D.C.

CHAPTER 16

Leaving Saigon the First Time

The explosion rattles my windows. I'm in my room at the Caravelle Hotel, sitting at the end of the bed when I hear it. I'm supposed to be resting from the miscarriage. I need to remain in the room until my dizziness ceases. But sitting in a room all day was never my style. It's even worse, considering that I have all this time to think. A few days before, I made an attempt to get out of my room on my own, if only to stretch my legs. It didn't turn out well.

I went to the Post Office at the Joint Operations Center across from the hotel. I was standing by the window with the mail in my hand from our American P.O. Box when I fainted. I remember sliding down the wall as G.I.s ran up to help me.

"Are you okay?"

"Yes, I'm fine."

I sat down on a bench. I felt very dizzy. Even though I told them I was fine, as I sat there I wasn't feeling any better, at least not very quickly. I recovered, but I still felt unwell. They could obviously tell that I was not in the best shape, and they hovered around me, as if I might keel over at any moment.

They must have called my husband because he suddenly walked into the Post Office. It had only been a few minutes. We were across from ABC News, so he didn't have far to go. He was worried and suggested I go back to bed.

Right after the miscarriage, I had started feeling really ill: I was always light-headed, dizzy, and nauseous, and it certainly wasn't getting better today. If I was fainting in public, then I probably should have stayed home.

Dick took me back to our suite, and I stayed in for the rest of the day. But the next morning was another story. I could not be a prisoner. However, I still felt dizzy whenever I stood up. This was a problem, and I worried that what I felt was more than a miscarriage. I just didn't think the recovery should last this long.

That's when a small group of Vietcong parked a taxi full of explosives outside the AFN (American Forces Network) building in Saigon. It was a French-made taxicab that looked like a VW Beetle. This was the same AFN that Dick had worked for back in Frankfurt. The VC soldiers left the car and walked away. I heard the explosion. You couldn't mistake the sound. I ran to the window and watched smoke rising over the city. I knew immediately that the AFN or something near there was hit. I could judge exactly where it was. This was just a continuance of the Tet Offensive, and I had to report the story. I already covered so many of the events leading up to the bombing that I couldn't let it go.

The main problem was that Dick worked right in our hotel, and many of the people who worked with him knew that I had fainted at the Post Office. Word spreads fast, especially with journalists when it's about journalists. So I didn't want to be seen.

I grabbed my tape recorder and camera and stepped into the hallway. Rather than use the elevator, where someone from ABC might catch me, I headed for the stairwell. Going down the stairs I only felt slightly dizzy. I kept going to the parking lot, where I kept my VW, and headed over to AFN.

I saw a huge crater in the street. The windows were blown out of many buildings surrounding the crater. Smoke was still rising, and there were charred hunks of metal at the bottom of the hole. Chunks of asphalt, dirt, and concrete littered the street. There were twenty or thirty Vietcong cornered. I parked the car as close as possible and ran toward the commotion. I was just a bit out of breath when I arrived. There, people in the streets were moving every which way. Some were walking away from the scene, and some were running, while others still attempted to go about their daily lives, just a few hundred feet from an open battle. Although there weren't many enemy combatants at this engagement, imagine if there were thirty soldiers in your city conducting a shooting war? War zones are always in places where people live. The locales may seem exotic in a newspaper or on a TV screen, but these are people's lives, and their well-being, and their homes, which are being destroyed. You can't be a reporter in a war zone and not quickly see the human face of it.

There was sporadic gunfire coming from the Saigon River, and I headed there. The South Vietnamese soldiers were already in the street and nearby buildings; the police were on scene as well.

Nguyen Loan, Chief of National Police, stood shouting to a group of his men. At this point, Loan was infamous. His picture was taken while he shot an unarmed and bound Vietcong in the head during the fighting in Cholon the month before. The photo was taken at the moment of impact by AP photographer Eddie Adams. It has become an iconic image of the Vietnam War. After this, and probably even before, the Chief of Police had an entirely antagonistic relationship with the press. He was a cruel man. I asked him once why he did it. He told me that if I were in his shoes, I would have done the same thing. But this isn't true, and I told him so.

Now he stood pointing to a building rumored to be a whorehouse. He said there were VC inside. Then his men moved toward the building. I fell in with another journalist. There was gunfire, and we ran for cover. The other journalist was right behind me. I got hit in the back by something. I didn't know what happened. It hit me with such force that it threw me down to the ground. I banged my shoulder on the rubble. I immediately got up and started yelling at the reporter behind me. I thought he had something to do with it. He looked at me and said, "Not me. You were probably hit by shrapnel."

When he said that, I was startled. But if I had been hit, then I should be bleeding. That's when I looked down and saw that a piece of shrapnel was embedded in the double leather strap that I used to hold my tape recorder. This piece of leather saved me from getting a very nasty wound in my back. There's no telling what that piece of shrapnel could have done to me.

Later in the same engagement, Loan lost one of his legs to machine gunfire. After that, he still remained a force in South Vietnam. He fled to the United States when the country fell.

By the time I returned to the hotel, Dick had already heard that I was out at AFN covering the explosion. Word spread fast in Saigon. He shook his head in exasperation.

He did not want me to get hurt, and the fact that I was still feeling dizzy and nauseous was not a good sign. Why should I go into battles when I just had a miscarriage and was experiencing side effects? I could understand his point of view, but I couldn't be laid out inside my room, especially when there was a story as big as the explosion at AFN. You have to understand that until Tet, we thought the Americans really were in control of things. Of course there were bombings in the city, but that was a different kind of action. At this point, the VC and NVA were trying to prove that they could reach the Americans wherever they were and on a massive scale. They couldn't hold their ground very often, but they could certainly take it, like the time at the Embassy, which until that point had been sacrosanct. Taking ground from the Americans had a huge news effect. This particular incident wasn't exactly taking ground from the Americans, but the large scale bombing of the American Forces Network was a story worth telling, and there was no way I wasn't going to cover it.

I continued feeling nauseous. Something was wrong, so I went to an Army doctor in Saigon. I wanted to find out why I was feeling like I did, and why I had what seemed to be a small lump in my stomach. The Army doctor was fresh from the States and totally ill-equipped to be diagnosing people on his own. Nevertheless, this was the position he held, and so I listened to him when he told me that I was suffering from a non-cancerous growth he called a myom, which could grow to be as big as a baby. He went on to say that it could grow for as long as three months and that I would have to wait until it either shrunk on its own or could be surgically removed.

We were set to leave for Hong Kong for R&R. This was April '68, and we were scheduled for our ten days of downtime. We could travel anywhere we wanted with free airline tickets that could take us as far as Australia. This wasn't a bad deal, except that I continued to suffer from the same symptoms. I decided to see a gynecologist in Hong Kong as soon as possible. In the city, we found a former British military doctor. I was apprehensive about my visit since my last two trips to the doctor had resulted in the diagnoses of miscarriage and a non-cancerous growth. There was no telling what this old doctor would find when he examined me. One thing was for sure: he had to be better than the rookie doctor in Saigon.

Of all the things I expected this British doctor to tell me, I had not expected him to tell me that I was pregnant.

"But I can't be. I had a miscarriage."

"You must have had twins and miscarried one of them. It's rare, but it happens. And you are certainly still pregnant."

I didn't know how to feel. I was relieved to know I wasn't carrying around some growth, and I was happy to know that I still had a baby. But after the last month I had, being diagnosed pregnant was a strange ending, to say the least. It also made me wonder how much longer I should remain a war correspondent. My husband and I discussed the possibility of my moving to Hong Kong on a more permanent basis to have the baby. This seemed like the most sensible approach to take. The only question was when should I move to Hong Kong. The idea, frankly, put me off. I liked Hong Kong as well as any place, maybe more than others, but I didn't want to find myself cooped up there. Certainly visiting Hong Kong was fine, but living there was a different story.

Of course, there was the question of leaving the war. The plain truth was that I didn't want to leave Vietnam. I liked it in Saigon at that time. And I was doing something I really loved. I felt I was conveying the truth about these scenes, which the people back in Germany deserved to hear. For the first time in my life, and for the first time in my career, I felt like I was really doing something worthwhile. I don't intend to sound cliché, or to inflate the journalistic ego, but journalists really do serve an important function by bringing the facts of modern events to people. Now that I had become a contributing part of this group, I had no intention of leaving. Yet I was not callous to the idea of having a child as some people may be. I wanted a child. I wanted to be a mom. It's just that I wanted both at the same time.

We decided to rent a house in Hong Kong beginning in the summer so that I could have somewhere to go as the pregnancy got further along. For the time being, though, I was sure as hell going to be in Saigon, or at least in Vietnam, reporting.

After Tet, and the near death experiences I had, I was already thinking about how dangerous the assignments would be. In other words, before Tet I felt as if I was invincible. After Nam O, Hue, being shot at on the Embassy roof, and the minefields, I knew I could get hurt. More importantly, I knew that I could get killed and that somebody would be reporting about me. This was the first time I dwelled on this fact, and it bothered me.

CHAPTER 17

Count Hasso Rüdt
von Collenberg

It was Sunday night. Explosions echoed in the warm spring darkness. Every Westerner, whether military, State Department, or journalist, woke with the noise and then scrambled to find out what was going on. In my case, I ran down the two flights to the ABC offices in the Caravelle. We had a police radio there, and a group of ABC reporters huddled around the radio, hoping to hear an explanation of what was happening. A few picked up the phone. Who knew what, and what happened? We didn't have to wait long. We heard the crackling over the radio. "Gunfire! We're under attack!" a voice said. There was fighting in Saigon. Now more explosions follow the shouts on the radio.

This was the beginning of the May offensive. VC and NVA troops were determined to let the Americans and world know that they were not going to quietly evaporate into the jungle. They were there to stay. All the body counts and macabre scenes of heavy bombing and high kill rates were not going to convince them to stop fighting. The fact that they could put Saigon under attack in this way was a message heard loud and clear.

In the dark morning hours, we learned that Tan Son Nhat Airport was under attack, and there were explosions close to the US Embassy and fighting in Cholon again. The city was not safe. I knew that my friend Count Hasso Rüdt von Collenberg, the Chargé d'Affaires for the German Embassy in Saigon, lived by the airport near the horse track. I also knew that fighting was heavy in the area. I wanted to get in touch with him. But calling over to the German Embassy got me nowhere. The phone just rang and rang. I started to worry about him. As the morning turned into afternoon and he hadn't turned up yet, I really began to fear what might have happened to him. Of course, he may have been unable to leave his house, but I realized this was wishful thinking

It had only been a month since I'd asked him to be my baby's godfather. He graciously accepted. We laughed a little about it. And it had only been a few days since last we spoke. We had recently gotten news of the German doctors who disappeared in Hue. The news was not good.

The VC took the doctors with them. One of the doctors' wives had her leg blown off by a grenade, and they dragged her along with them. She must have been in terrible pain. Suddenly, they stopped in a field and killed the whole group.

Why would they have done that? This was a group of doctors who helped anyone regardless of what side of the war they were on. Yet this group of Vietcong shot them, as if they were the enemy.

This was the topic Hasso Rüdt and I were discussing a few days before the May offensive. Hasso Rüdt was of the opinion that the doctors were shot because they allowed themselves to be taken out of the city. Had they remained where they were, the Vietcong would not have killed them. It seemed as if there was a certain logic to his theory. The idea was that they wouldn't kill you outside the heat of battle if you were a civilian in a populated area. It was unthinkable that they would do such a thing.

It was at the Five-O'Clock Follies that I heard from our Vietnamese/German translator that a dead Caucasian was found in Cholon. He leaned in and asked me, "Do you think it could be Hasso Rüdt von Collenberg?"

"Oh my God, don't say that too loudly here."

I knew Hasso Rüdt, and I didn't want to make this a story. I didn't want to upset his family. What if it wasn't true, and people reported it? Right then I was determined to find out the truth.

First, I rushed to the Continental Hotel. Word had already spread like wildfire. The German correspondents were all talking about it. I was worried about this because I didn't want anyone to rush out with a story. That would be awful. It wasn't unheard of for people to be reported dead in war zones when they were perfectly fine. Such is the nature of reporting: sometimes people go to print with stories when they don't have enough information to support their case. It's often the sense of competition that drives this knee-jerk reaction to report before all the facts are confirmed. I wanted to avoid that. If it really was Hasso Rüdt von Collenberg lying in the field hospital, then I wanted his family to be notified before they read it in a newspaper.

I took the German press attaché aside and spoke with him: "I've been told there's a dead Caucasian in the 3rd field hospital by Tan Son Nhat. Would you like to come with me to investigate?" He agreed.

We took his Beetle and drove to the field hospital. We searched for him, but he wasn't there. Then we were directed to another field hospital across town. After last night's attack, the city was not a safe place to drive. My husband at ABC had even issued an order to keep everyone inside. There still were isolated pockets of fighting. Aside from the known areas of combat, you never knew when you might encounter a group of VC, who simply would attack you for being a Caucasian in Saigon. People were kidnapped all the time. Dick and I already had had several friends killed.

We reached the 5th Field Hospital. We saw an ambulance parked beneath an old archway in the driveway. They had not gotten around to bringing in the body, and the driver was nowhere to be found. I asked if there was a Caucasian body. "Yeah, it's in the ambulance," someone replied. When they let us inside, we found Hasso Rüdt von Collenberg dead from gunshot wounds. He was blindfolded, and the bandana was soaked in blood.

When I saw him, I told the German press attaché not to release the story until his family was notified. "Put a lid on this until we get to his family!" Of course, he agreed.

Soon after that, I learned where he was shot. I went to the scene to learn what I could about his death. What I found was frightening. Apparently he had left his home near the airport when the fighting began. He drove toward Cholon. My guess is that he was trying to see what was going on.

I had a Vietnamese translator with me. Together we found several eyewitnesses. The first group was two women who described what they saw until he turned off the road where they stood. They saw his Beetle come down the street headed for the fighting, which was just up ahead. When he saw that, he tried to turn around and go back the way he had come. Just ahead of him before the fighting, there was a short connector road that turned back in the direction he wanted to go. The problem was that there were two young VC soldiers standing on the road. The women saw Hasso Rüdt making the turn and tried their best to wave him off. But he must not have seen them.

The next eyewitness was a South Vietnamese Lieutenant who lived on the connector road. When Hasso Rüdt made his turn, the two young VC soldiers pointed their AK-47s at him.

They saw that he was a Westerner. Therefore, he was a target. They ordered him to get out of the car. He showed them his diplomatic papers. Apparently, they didn't care. Talking between themselves the whole time, they decided to blindfold him. After that, they continued to talk. Then there was an explosion on the street, possibly mortar fire from the fighting close to where they stood. When the explosion occurred, one of the Vietcong raised his assault rifle on full automatic, firing as he lifted his hand. The first two shots struck Hasso Rüdt in the buttocks. The next shot entered just behind his left ear and killed him. The car door was still open, and the motor was running. An ambulance arrived to collect his body at 2:30 in the afternoon.

I later learned that someone had run the story without any facts and before his family was notified.

The senselessness of his murder bothered me. They obviously didn't have to kill him. And it was because he decided to turn onto a street rather than doing a U-turn on the road he was on. Had he done that, the would-be godfather of my child would be alive.

It was just after the shooting that I began having nightmares. I had not had such frightening dreams since I was a child. As a girl just after the war, I dreamt of falling into holes night after night. It was a recurring dream.

Now when I slept, I dreamt of being in a Vietnamese hut. I was looking toward a kitchen when suddenly VC were coming out of a tunnel in the ground, which I hadn't noticed. They were everywhere and flooding the kitchen. There was nowhere to go. I couldn't hide. I couldn't run. I was doomed. And I would have this nightmare again and again.

The same day Hasso Rüdt was killed, three other journalists were killed in a Jeep driving out to Cholon. One escaped; the rest were shot. It was getting hairy in Saigon. You had to be really careful what corner you turned down. I still didn't want to leave. It was beyond the feeling of doing something important at this point. I liked what I did here, and I didn't want to give it up. But at the same time, I became more careful. Being pregnant helped to change the way I thought. It especially changed the way I thought about vaccination. We always were taking vaccinations. Fearing what they might do to my unborn child, I stopped taking them altogether. I just started rolling down my sleeves to protect myself from mosquitoes. To avoid the other vaccinations I was supposed to take on a regular basis, I simply found a doctor who was willing to issue a note saying he had administered them. I was willing to run the risk of getting a horrible disease because I thought the vaccines could be worse for the baby. And they would have been.

Despite all this, the time for me to leave was drawing near. It was also time for Dick to go. By this point, we had been in Saigon for almost two years. Ideally, they wanted to keep Bureau Chiefs in country no longer than a year since it was a hard position. We already had begun preparing mentally for the move. We knew that it was coming at the end of the year when the new Bureau Chief was slated to arrive. I was happy at the idea of leaving. It would be a relief, and yet I still had the nagging sense that I wanted to remain. Of course, before we could head back to the States, I was scheduled to give birth in a Hong Kong hospital.

One of the last stories I covered before leaving Saigon involved a quick flight down to the Delta to report on the aftermath of some fighting that happened the day before. I picked up the story through MACV. It was routine, and the flight wouldn't put me in harm's way. The story I covered there has remained with me all these years, nonetheless. When I returned to Vietnam to film a documentary for German Television in the 1980s, I recalled what I had seen to one of our tour guides. He was busy reminding me of the atrocities the Americans had perpetrated. Maybe so, but they had never done anything like this.

Fleeing from American forces, the Vietcong left a group of five Vietnamese boys tied up together in a rice paddy. The rope was tied around each of their necks. Between them they had a single AK-47. The idea was that one or two boys might run away. But five tied together, in terror of the Americans, would stand and fight, at least until the American G.I.s stopped them. And this is what the VC did in order to give themselves covering fire. Behind this fire, they escaped into the bush. I was appalled to see the five dead boys all tied up, lying in the wet field. This wasn't even what the MACV people thought to show me. The story was about how the Americans had pushed the Vietcong back. I don't remember the specifics. I just remember the boys and thinking, "How cruel could they be?" I also learned that this was not the first time the Vietcong had used this tactic. I was shown several other examples of the same behavior, which had happened in the previous day's engagement. While not common, it happened with enough frequency that the men there had all seen it. This horror was apparently a popular Vietcong strategy.

In July, I moved into the house we rented in Hong Kong. It was a lovely single-family house. We called it the White House because it resembled the White House back in D.C., only much smaller. It was in the hillside above a place called Happy Valley, which was the racetrack. None of it exists any longer; they tore it down and built two high-rises.

Despite how nice it was there, I couldn't spend all my time waiting to give birth in such a large house without doing something. It had never been my nature to sit still, and I wasn't going to begin then.

Of course, there was no war to report on, and since all of my friends were in Saigon, I did the most logical thing I could think of. I had furniture made. Handmade furniture was readily available in Hong Kong, and all I had to do was to pick out what I wanted, and they made it for me. I couldn't have been happier with that.

I returned one time to Saigon before my son was born. This was right after a typhoon hit Hong Kong. The plane ahead of us crashed on the runway, and the accident turned into an irritating comedy of bureaucratic errors. It took longer to get into the air. When we were finally airborne, we weren't allowed to land in Saigon because of the curfew. We landed in Bangkok instead. But we didn't have a visa for

Bangkok. The man at customs said, "What do you want here? You don't have a visa."

I said, "I don't want to be here. I want to be in Saigon. But they won't take us because there's a curfew."

You might have thought they would have known this, since our flight had not been scheduled to land here in the first place. But apparently one hand didn't know what the other was doing. It got worse. The airline put us up for the night. In the morning, there were new customs people who asked the same questions.

"No visa, no visa," they said. "What is the purpose of your visit?"

"Necessity," I said.

We finally got to Saigon, and our cameraman had arranged a special dinner for me. He had even typed up a menu, which was very nice. Everyone from ABC was there. My husband was getting antsy, though. He asked me how long I was planning to stay. He was worried, I guess, that I might give birth. But I told him not to worry. It wasn't time yet. I had already made up my mind that I was going to give birth on October 10th. I'm German so when I make up my mind about something, it happens. And in this case, it did.

On October 10th, 1968, I gave birth to my son Peter in a Hong Kong hospital that was more comfortable than many hotels I've been in.

CHAPTER 18

Chicago

Washington D.C. promised to be a pleasant break from Saigon. Dick and I were looking forward to settling in to raise our new son in the capital. And we had the money to buy a house. We were a little upset that we wouldn't be able to see David and Martha. After all, they had moved to Chicago after David's tour of duty to work in his family's printing business. We resolved to take our vacations with them, which gave us some consolation. We had become very close with them in Saigon. We didn't get to see Martha as often since she lived in Bangkok. She and I were friends despite the distance, and we would continue to be even though we were separated by thousands of miles.

On a Sunday afternoon not too long after returning from Hong Kong, we finally decided on a house just outside of D.C. We signed the papers that day. We were now homeowners.

But on Monday morning Dick learned from ABC that he was named Bureau Chief in Chicago, effective immediately. Such is life at the networks, and if you want to keep moving in the company, you go where they need you to be. So we put the house we just bought, but never lived in, up for rent and moved into an apartment near Lake Michigan in Evanston. The move was inconvenient, but we did get to live near David and Martha, which made the city seem much more friendly to us since we already had friends there. We became even closer then. I even potty trained their son Adam.

Martha was having trouble teaching him that. I said, "Give him to me, I can teach him." In my opinion, boys are much harder to potty train than girls. But Adam spent the weekend with me. He was nearly three years old. I was very persistent with him. After the weekend was over, he really did know how to use the toilet. Martha and David were so happy. They took him to a movie. Afterward, they called me up. Martha said, "He really does know how. He told us when he had to go and everything." I was very proud of myself.

We soon made many new friends in Chicago. I had the advantage of being married to ABC's Bureau Chief, which at the time meant that I accompanied Dick to parties in the city. Pretty soon, Hugh Hefner of *Playboy* invited us over to "The Mansion" for one of his parties. He had a pool and a grotto in his basement; it was very cool. He would have these get-togethers a couple times a week, and we got to be very friendly with Hefner. Back then, *Playboy* was as much a cultural and intellectual magazine as anything else. You really could make the claim that you read it for the articles. Because of this cultural cache, the *Playboy* parties drew an interesting set. This crowd gave me access to a world that I could write about.

Of course, there were no Five O'Clock Follies or MACV stories in Chicago. Here the story always changed, while in Saigon the story was the war. If I was persistent, I could find something worth writing about that my editor back in Germany would want to read. In this way, the parties at Hef's could work for me almost like MACV.

Right away, I decided to write about what it was like to be a bunny at the Playboy Clubs. This wasn't the most absorbing topic I could think of, but it was interesting—a nice break from war—and I thought they would accept my story back in Germany because it was a little salacious. I asked permission from *Playboy* to let me do the story. I wanted to write this piece in the same way I had written my Vietnam pieces. That meant it would be a first-person narrative of what it was like to go through the training. Hef agreed to let me interview some of the girls and see what they endured.

I'll tell you, their job wasn't easy. The training consisted of learning to be a waitress while walking around in a tight and revealing bathing suit, which they called "bunny suits." I wanted no part of wearing that thing. And while I typically went through whatever my subjects went through, I took a pass in putting on a bunny suit. In the end, taking a pass didn't really matter, as the newspaper that ran the story chose to superimpose bunny ears on a picture of me and run it that way. I wasn't sure if I should be mad or laugh. I chose the latter, and moved on to the next story.

We often went to the Mansion for *Playboy* parties. But the word "party" makes these get-togethers seem like more than they were. They were often for business, and they weren't usually a formal "to-do." Guests would play poker—it was that sort of atmosphere. And did I know how to play poker. But at the Mansion, we played "Dollar-Bill-Poker," which is not a card game at all. You just bet on the serial numbers on a dollar bill, and whoever bets correctly wins.

Hef would come out in his bathrobe, which he always wore. We usually stood in a circle around his living room (which was more like a banquet hall) clutching our dollar bills. Hef always wanted to play, but he never had any cash on him. He was always asking to borrow dollar bills, then he wouldn't pay them back. After this happened more than once, I told him that he should ask his own people for a loan. I wasn't going to play poker against someone I just lent the money to, and besides, we were in his mansion. He was happy like a little boy when he won, maybe because it was always on borrowed money.

I met Jesse Jackson at one of these gatherings. I don't remember the event in all its particulars, but I do remember that he called me a "blue-eyed devil." We were dancing at the time, and he was wearing a Hawaiian shirt. When he called me that, I responded, "And you are dancing with this blue-eyed devil." Years later, when he was running for President, I covered him on the campaign trail. When I reminded him of his comment, he replied, "Oh, I would never say that."

"Yeah, sure," I said, "But you did."

At that time, Jessie Jackson wasn't very well-known. He was with Martin Luther King when he was assassinated, but people were not really talking about him after that. Well, Hef had taken a liking to him and was helping him. Hef would invite him to his big events, and he would take Jesse out on stage and introduce him. The exposure, you can be sure, helped out Mr. Jackson's career to no small degree.

I met George Plimpton there as well. I was so happy to meet him because I based many of my reporting ideas on his style. Plimpton was very famous at that time. He would put himself in crazy scenarios and then write about them. He became a professional football player and got beaten up quite a bit, and he loved every minute of it. I always had enjoyed his stories and wanted to do the same thing. I told him how much he meant to me and that he was something of an idol. He seemed pleased when I said, "I live the story and then write about it."

By this point, I was coming into my own. I had handled several stories already and was enjoying it. I never had any difficulty getting new material to write about. If I thought up something interesting then I did it, and the DPA Special Service in Germany would pick up my magazine-length pieces. I could do what I wanted. If I wanted to see what it was like to be a firefighter, I went out on the story, although that's not really the way it happened. I managed to get access to "His Honor," Mayor Richard Dailey of Chicago, for another story. He was good to me, and we had our picture taken together. Then he told me about his Fire Department. He called it *his* Fire Department. He was proud of how they performed and told me that I should do a story on them. His Honor put me in touch with someone, who arranged to have me spend three nights with the Fire Department. The station was in Cabrini Greens, a high-rise slum that straddled Millionaires Row on Lake Michigan.

The first night, the firefighters let me ride on the side of the engine on the way to a fire. I thought it would be a great thrill to ride on the back of a big rig. In reality, it was anything but enjoyable. The gloves they gave me were too big, so I couldn't hang on to the metal handles. I took the gloves off. It was March in Chicago and bitterly cold. My hands were frozen within a minute, but I had to hold on. The streets were in rough shape, and driving around on them while I stood on the side of the truck was no treat.

What I learned, aside from not to ride on the side of a truck ever again, is how dangerous their job is and how brave they are. They took me into a single-family house with them. I was wearing a helmet, but I didn't have on any type of SCBA (Self-Contained-Breathing-Apparatus) or other equipment. The fire was on the second floor, and they pulled the ceiling down. They had long bars with hooked ends and they gave one to me and had me pull the ceiling with them. It wasn't fun. The smoke got to me. Something kicked up, and the room got too smoky so that I couldn't breathe. I had to leave the room, and it took me several minutes to recover. I have a great deal of respect for firefighters because of that, and also got a glimpse of what it's like to die in a smoke-filled building. I wanted no part of that.

The next day I brought my son over with me. He was around three years old. Of course, he wanted to see the fire engine. And so they took him up on the truck. All of a sudden, the siren went off. I was standing in the garage and the truck, which was in the driveway, just started up and left with my son riding right inside. I was frantic. I shouted to them, but they didn't stop. Then the truck disappeared around the corner. I thought that Peter could be in worse hands than with firefighters. Of course, they wouldn't let him off the truck if they actually did go to a fire. "Dear God, don't let them leave my son alone," I thought.

In a few minutes they returned, laughing. They had done it as a joke to mess with me. Peter, however, had a great time riding that great big red engine down the streets, pulling the cord for the siren. It was the coolest adventure of his young life.

During my Chicago period, I wanted to do a story on John Johnson. I had read several stories about him. He was the richest black man in America. He was the publisher of *Ebony* and *Jet Magazine*. He agreed to an interview. When I got there, it wasn't Johnson who was there but his managing editor Hans Massaquoi. When he introduced himself, I said, "Well, Hans sounds like a German name if I ever heard one."

"I am half German," he said. Then he told me his life story. Hans' mother was German. His grandfather was the general counsel for Liberia in Hamburg, Germany, and his father was a Liberian diplomat. His parents were married in Hamburg. Hans was born there just before the war. Hans' father returned to Liberia. He told his wife that she could go with him, but she declined. She was a nurse and wanted to stay in Hamburg. Hans stayed with her. It was a very interesting adventure to grow up as a black child in Nazi Germany, to say the least. He made it through the whole war under the Nazis and then moved away.

After telling me his story, Hans gave me lots of inside stories on Johnson and the inner workings of his publishing empire. I told some of the stories in my article. I also wrote that John Johnson had the mentality of a benevolent plantation owner because that's how he treated his management team. I still think it's true. When he would get angry with Hans, Johnson would say, "I pay you like a white man; I expect you to work like one."

When I published the article, Hans, who had read it in German, called me up and asked me why I had written that Johnson was like a benevolent plantation owner.

"Don't you know he's going to have me translate it to him?"

"Well, don't translate that part," I told him.

Hans must have accurately translated it because I learned that John Johnson was not happy about what I wrote. Hans didn't hold it against me, though. After that, Hans would call and try to entice me with lurid stories. He wanted me to come over to his apartment. He would say things like, "My neighbors are very loud. One neighbor is a screamer, and the other is a moaner. You should come over and hear them." Once he told me that he knew German girls were the best in bed and he would give me the chance to prove it to him. Of course, I replied, "If you already know we are the best, then why do I have to prove it to you?" On another occasion, he told me, "The rumors about how blacks are hung are not all true, but they are pretty close." He also tried telephone sex, but I just had to giggle. I thought it was hilarious.

We actually became close friends. Much later, Hans wrote a book called *Destined to Witness,* which became very famous in Germany and made Hans very famous. After his sudden fame, he asked whether I thought he should go to a certain area in Germany. I told him that he shouldn't because he was black. He was hurt to hear this, as he had a right to be. He said he almost never felt unsafe as a young man growing up under the Nazis and now, in 2000, he couldn't go to the country of his childhood because of color, even though he was culturally German.

Many of the stories and the people I covered were very interesting in this period. I was the first woman to ride NASA's Lunar Module Simulator, and I was the first woman on a nuclear submarine. I also become a clown at Barnum and Bailey Circus. After attending "Clown College," they let me come out into the arena dressed in clown makeup. My son Peter came to the auditorium that day. When I came up to him in the stands, he thought I was one of the clowns. But then I said, "Hi, Peter." He recognized his mother's voice but not my face. He started to cry.

This time also helped me to progress as a writer outside of my Vietnam writing. Although we had moved away, Vietnam was not out of the picture. In 1970, Dick was asked to fill in as ABC's Bureau Chief in Saigon again. One of my cousins was staying with us in Chicago and helping to take care of Peter. I decided to take a three-month trip back to see what I could learn. I learned that it was not the country I remembered—and also, to never get into a jet with a South Vietnamese flyboy.

CHAPTER 19

Back to Vietnam

In the spring of 1970, we returned to Vietnam. I was only there for three months. Right off the bat, you could see the country was different. The Americans were mounting their *Vietnamization* campaign in an effort to turn over control to the South Vietnamese. They were trying to pull out at this point, and mostly advisors remained. I thought it was a lost cause.

At the same time the Americans were *Vietnamizing* Vietnam, they were also venturing openly into Cambodia on military missions. By 1970, the Cambodian army was fighting the Khmer Rouge, which was the Communist party in Cambodia. They were actively trying to take over the country and were naturally allied with the North Vietnamese. At that point, the United States military was officially allowed to root out the Communists in Cambodia by finding and destroying their headquarters in the jungle. The Americans were also still trying to locate the hub of the Ho Chi Minh trail, where the military thought the VC had a base. (This was the area by the old rubber plantation, where I inadvertently ran across a minefield.)

Among the stories I wanted to cover when I got back into the country was the American foray into Cambodia. This same military reality also attracted journalists Dana Stone and Sean Flynn, who were both killed in Cambodia. They were too brazen.

Dana Stone was a freelance cameraman for CBS and a freelance photographer for the AP. He was out of the country until the

Americans announced they were entering Cambodia, and then he decided he had to be there to document what was taking place. He had a young wife who lived in Hong Kong and Saigon. Dana had very poor eyesight and wore thick glasses. I always thought that was sort of funny, as he was a photographer.

Sean Flynn was tall, blond, and drop-dead gorgeous. He was the son of American actor Errol Flynn. I believe he was trying to live up to his father, who had already passed away. My husband and others warned me about him: "Stay away from him. He's real trouble." He was looking for action and seemed to have a death wish. He carried weapons, and I stayed away from him for that reason alone.

They left from Phnom Penh one morning on their Hondas and never returned. They couldn't wait along with the rest of us, who were flying to the capital together. It was April 6, 1970 when they left. They were never seen again.

Before I got into Cambodia, another opportunity presented itself. Whenever I asked to take a flight in a fighter jet on my previous tour in country, the American PIOs (Public Information Officer) would never let me do it. The Lieutenant Colonel even said, "I wouldn't let my own daughter go up in one of those things." And that's pretty much how things stood.

But now there was a new PIO officer at MACV. He had no qualms about letting me go up in a jet. In fact, he was happy to show off his South Vietnamese pilots. "These pilots are really great," he said. He had one particular pilot in mind. "Come down to the Delta, and you can go up in a trainer with him." The trainers had side-by-side seats in the cockpits, so you could sit with the pilot, which was exactly what I wanted.

I was excited to go. I brought my camera. I had been trying to get on one of these flights for years. Now the opportunity was here.

I went down to the Delta before we left for Cambodia. The base was near Can Tho, which was surrounded by rice paddies. I climbed into a plane with a very cocky South Vietnamese flyboy. He made the Americans at Pleiku look tame. This pilot seemed as eager to show off to me as the PIO had been.

We went down the runway for takeoff. Before the plane got off the ground, I started getting hit with hot air from the vent next to my side. It was so hot that it was burning me. I turned to the pilot, "There's hot air coming in here."

"It must be engine air. Push the vent away from you."

I tried, but it was so hot I couldn't touch it. Now we were headed down the runway, and I was trying to get away from the air and was putting whatever I had in front of me to block the airflow. Nothing was working, and I could only move a few inches in my restraints.

"Can't you stop the plane?"

"Too late. Too late," he said. "We have to take off."

I guess we wouldn't have stopped in time before the end of the runway. We took off, and there was a metallic noise. I thought whatever was causing the hot air now had broken in the engine and was going to send us down. I don't know if the pilot found it or if it regulated itself once we were airborne, but the hot air stopped and the flight was smooth.

It really had been engine air, which can reach several hundred degrees. I later learned I had second-degree burns all over my right leg and arm, which really hurt. I wasn't eager to keep going, but the pilot had to do his bombing run. On the return flight, since everything had gone so well during takeoff, he decided to show me what the plane could do and how close these planes could fly to each other.

"No, you don't have to show me," I said.

"Oh, I show you. I show you. I can go one inch to his wing." He pointed to the jet flying near to us now in formation.

I said to myself: "Oh God, he's not doing this." But sure enough, he was. I almost could have reached out and touched the other wing. They were right there. I was thinking, "We're going to die, for sure. This guy is out to kill us. My poor little son; he's going to grow up without his mother." I turned my camera around and took a picture of myself. Of course, all you could see was the helmet and the oxygen mask, but if we died at least I wanted to have a picture of my last moments.

When he was done with the air show, I said, "Thank you. I'm really glad you showed me all your skills. Now can we land?" And we did just that. I guess the presentation was over. We taxied down the runway and stopped the plane by a hanger. I stepped down the ladder.

On the ground, I saw the Lieutenant Colonel, the PIO who had let me go up. He took me in his arms when he saw me. "You're really here."

"Yeah, of course we're here."

"I saw you guys going up. Did you realize that your wheel hit one of the trees at the end of the runway?"

"No," I said, "We had so many problems during takeoff I didn't notice that."

"I was already making up stories to tell MACV. What was I going to tell Saigon? That I let a reporter crash and die on a plane? I'm so glad you came back alive."

"Well, I'm sure glad you came up with the idea that I should fly with your best South Vietnamese pilot."

Since I was being scalded by hot air from the engine, the pilot probably wasn't paying as much attention as he should have to the takeoff. We didn't get enough speed, and he hit the tops of one of the trees with the landing gear. We should have crashed, but this guy was either really good or lucky because he got us out of it. I hadn't even noticed there was a problem.

After that I thought, "I really can't do this kind of stuff anymore. Thea, you have a son you have to think about. You are a mother."

But the Americans were making a big push into Cambodia. I told myself it was not dangerous because so many journalists were taking the trip in together and there was security in numbers. I just had to be there. This was the main story, and if you were any kind of a journalist in country, you had to go to Cambodia. The Americans were finally making an official foray into the neighboring country, and that was it.

And so I went. I took a commercial flight with my husband and a slew of other journalists to Phnom Phen in Cambodia, which is close to the border with Vietnam in the south. The idea that we were flying in also gave me some comfort.

The U.S. offensive was not far from Phnom Phen; we were able to drive to the action. We trekked out to see the fighting just a few days after we landed. In the meantime, I thought I might use my German citizenship to talk with the East German Press Attaché. There was no West German Press Attaché at that time in Cambodia. I contacted him primarily to see if he had any information on the missing journalists. I was happy when he agreed to speak with me.

In fact, he invited me over to his house. He was very polite when I arrived. He offered me some cognac, and I accepted. We sat at a table and drank together. After our initial small talk ended, I began asking him about Flynn and Stone. I didn't know if they were dead. It seems most likely they were still alive at that point, and they were kept alive for a year before they were killed.

I was pressing the East German Press Attaché for any information he might have that could help with their release. He said, "I don't know anything about where they are. All I know is that they've been taken."

Then I suddenly began to feel dizzy and light-headed. I was going to faint. I'm thinking, "Oh God, this man has drugged me with his cognac." He was obviously a spy of some sort.

He saw that I didn't feel well and offered to drive me back to the hotel. But I was a West German. I knew horror stories about East German spies. I didn't believe he was going to help me. I thought he was taking me somewhere else. If he took me in any direction other than toward my hotel, I would run for my life. I just didn't know if I had the strength to run away.

As it turned out, the car ride was good for me, and he had no intention of kidnapping me. I began to feel better. I really don't know what caused me to feel that way. I apologized to him. Just then, he turned on the radio, and Cambodia's Prime Minister Sihanouk was giving a speech. He was in exile in China at the time. At one point or another, he held every title under the sun in Cambodia, including King and Prime Minister.

The East German Press Attaché listened to his speech intently. He could speak Cambodian. It was very long, going on and on and saying all these positive things about the Americans. That's when the Press Attaché turned to me and said, "That's not Sihanouk. He would never say that. I know his speeches. And that is not him."

"What do you mean?"

"It's probably the CIA."

"They can do that? How?" I asked him.

"Oh yes," he said confidently, "It is meticulous work. They need hundreds of speeches and they splice them all together."

"Oh, you must know how this works."

I thought he probably had some experience in doing this with people's speeches. I also made a mental note to check out this possibility with someone I knew in the CIA when I got back to Saigon.

In a few minutes, he dropped me at my hotel. We said our goodbyes. The car ride had been interesting indeed. But I couldn't focus on the CIA story at the moment, for now it was time for us to see if we could reach the Offensive.

We headed out the following day. All the journalists set out from the capital into the jungle to try to meet up with the American Offensive. The idea was to get some sense of what the Offensive was achieving. The further we drove into the steamy jungle, the more difficult it became to travel. Have you ever seen what a bomb dropped from the air does to a road? Let alone, hundreds of them? It didn't make the drive easy. The place was destroyed. The road was shot full with craters. All the bridges were blown out, but here and there we drove over heavy timbers which were placed across the blown-out spans.

We reached a bridge that was utterly impassable by car. It just couldn't be done, and so we had to cross on foot. But we could only go across this river in single file. That's when one of the reporters from CBS—I won't say his name—started to get angry with me. He said, "Why do you go first? Why don't you let someone else cross ahead of you? You're not even a journalist. You're just the wife of a Bureau Chief. You have no business being here."

"I am a correspondent for the German Press Agency. I've been all over . . ."

I was going to say something further to him, but before I could utter another word, one of the ABC correspondents dug into him, "This *girl* has been through more action than you'll ever go through, and has become better known through her writing than you ever will be in any of your reporting. So I'd keep my mouth shut."

He didn't say another word to me. When we got to the other side, I said to the ABC correspondent, "Thank you for that, Steve, and you've never even read my stories. They are in German." He just laughed. It was Steve Bell, who would later become an anchor on *Good Morning America*. From there, we walked on to a paved road. I was walking when we received fire from the side of the road. We tried to crawl forward but then decided to turn back. The Americans hadn't made the inroads they'd hoped. It all just seemed like more senseless destruction to us. Everybody reported it that way. Then we returned to Saigon.

I thought I might at least get one interesting story there, so I followed up on the idea of the CIA splicing together the Sihanouk speech. I met with the CIA Station Chief. I asked this spook if he knew about the splicing. He said, "Of course not. We wouldn't do a thing like that, and if we did, do you think I would tell you?"

"No, you don't have to tell me anything. You just have to confirm something." I worded my questions so he just had to confirm or deny what I said. "Would you deny that this is possible?"

"No."

"Would that be a "no comment" if I said that you could actually splice his speeches?"

"Yes."

"Was Sihanouk known to say these words? Isn't it true that he never said any pro-American words in a speech?"

"Yes."

In a roundabout way, I got him to confirm that the CIA had spliced this speech together. At the end of the interview, I said to him, "You did a terrific job because that was a very long speech. I have to say. I wonder if the Cambodians went for it because I can tell you the East German Press Attaché didn't. He knew what it was immediately."

He said, "You know they accuse us of a lot of things."

"And sometimes they are true." That's what I reported.

CHAPTER 20

Washington D.C.

I was standing on the tarmac at Andrews Air Force Base just outside of Washington D.C. Dick was about to arrive, and I was waiting for him. He had been traveling with President Ford on a campaign trip. It was 1976, an election year. Ford was on his way to losing to Jimmy Carter for the Presidency, but that was still to come.

We had been in D.C. for just a few months since moving from Los Angeles. When ABC asked us to move, we had little choice in the matter. From Chicago we were sent to L.A. We were supposed to remain there, but suddenly, just a few months into our stay, they had us move again. At least they gave us more time and even kindly allowed me to have my daughter in the hospital with the doctor I had become accustomed to.

Even in that short time, I managed to do several stories. One of them focused on the women of the Ku Klux Klan, who were involved mostly because they were attracted to David Duke. They were like his groupies. They said as much. It was very strange. I even got to interview Duke himself just outside of New Orleans. The Klansmen would always meet with me because I was German. I guess they thought I was some kind of Nazi. They assumed "Rosenbaum" was a German name. Whatever they thought about me didn't change the way I reported on them.

Duke and I met in a restaurant. The waiter was black. I asked, "Does he know who you are?"

"Yes, of course he knows who I am. He knows better than to do anything about it."

That wasn't the only time I did a story on the Klan. German audiences seemed fascinated by this strange American cult, so I did many stories on the Klan over the years.

My daughter, Petra, was born February 25th, 1975. By the end of March, we moved out of L.A. We had made the trip to Washington once before, right after we first left Vietnam. At least on this move, we would get to live in the house we bought. My mother came in from Germany to watch the children. This allowed me time to go house hunting.

I resumed my freelancing activities right away after moving to Washington. By now, I had built up a client list and was writing under various names for the weekly magazines that came inside newspapers while also sending back other stories for publication in Germany. But I wasn't on the tarmac staring at Air Force One for my writing. Today, I was simply a wife here to pick up her husband.

I was early and had both kids with me. My daughter was just an infant, and my son was six. Air Force One had just arrived, which meant the tarmac was frozen and nobody from the press plane could disembark. Because I had the time, I thought it would be nice to get a glimpse of President Ford as he came off the plane.

However, a number of people had the same idea. We all wandered onto the tarmac. When President Ford walked over to us, the group encircled him. I had Petra in my arms and Peter by the hand. Everyone pushed forward. I got stuck in the crowd, and suddenly, my son was gone.

I didn't panic right away, but I certainly didn't feel comfortable with the fact. I knew that he wanted to see the President, so I began to push my way to the front.

I was afraid of causing an alarm with the President, and I felt somewhat embarrassed. Under any other circumstance, I would have behaved differently, but with the President there, I didn't want to shout for Peter. All the same, I had a sinking feeling because there's really no telling where a little boy might run off to, or what he might see that could send him in a new direction.

I didn't see Peter anywhere. Now I was really nervous. "Where could he be?" I kept saying his name. And then I heard the President and his entourage. Finally, I made it to the front and saw Ford walking around the circle of people, shaking hands. My son Peter was holding onto Ford's other hand. He smiled benevolently and waved. Ford seemed to think that was perfectly normal. He probably thought Peter was the son of a staffer. The crowd must have assumed Peter was somehow related to Mr. Ford.

When the President finished his "meet and greet," he turned to my son, shook his hand and said, "Thanks for helping me out here, Peter." Peter said his goodbyes and happily skipped over to his relieved mother.

"I told you not to go with strangers," I said when he returned.

"But he's not a stranger, Mom. He's the President."

I won't forget that as long as I live. Nothing happened, of course, beyond Peter escaping and joining the President as he shook hands. Still, it was more memorable for me and my children than many of the stories I worked on then. How often does the President take a strange child by the hand? And that child is yours. This incident also related to my freelance life because the presidential campaign was underway. I hadn't been there for a story. But if I had, I would have tried to get Ford to talk about his opponent at the time, who seemed to be gaining steam, and doing so with a down-to-earth style.

That was the story on so many of my clients' minds. Carter was the Governor of Georgia and running for President. Of course, everyone wanted an interview with him. I was somewhat handicapped in getting to him because I was German. Why would an American presidential candidate care what a freelance writer for mostly German magazines thought of him? Through a contact I had made in Vietnam, I got to Jody Powell. He was working as Carter's Press Secretary for the campaign. He had the same question: "Why do I want to give a German writer an interview with the presidential candidate? How many votes will my candidate get in Germany?"

"Because you have G.I.s in Germany who will vote. And some of them may read the story that I will do on him. And you can never think about foreign policy early enough."

He must have accepted my argument, or at least he caved in to my persistence, because he gave me access to his candidate. He knew I was serious since I had traveled to Carter's hometown of Plains, Georgia, just to meet with him and to hang around campaign headquarters for hours on end where it was oppressively hot.

I met Jimmy Carter in his house. The formal furniture at this southern ranch surprised me, and he didn't exactly look like a man who was finishing a four-week vacation at home. Beads of sweat had formed on his forehead in the heat of the day. Red blotches emphasized the paleness of his face. He shook my hand. Despite the heat, his hand was not sweaty. The grip was friendly. But he didn't honor me with his famous toothy grin. Then again, I wasn't a potential voter, and this former submarine captain and peanut farmer from the south, who was at that time running hard, didn't waste his time and gestures so easily.

When he did laugh, he only laughed up to his nose. His light blue eyes could have hardened a melting ice cream cone in the 90-degree heat. That day he wore his standard uniform: jeans and a jean shirt with checkered appliqué. His dark brown, well-worn, sturdy shoes were made to walk through peanut fields.

He seemed easy-going enough, walking here and there to be photographed. He wouldn't sit down in his daughter's hammock, though. "That won't hold me; it's Amy's." The hammock looked sturdy enough, but surely Carter knew that hammocks tended to make their occupants look ridiculous and, if slightly unbalanced, turned you over altogether.

Carter knew what made him look good on television. There were countless pictures and miles of film showing him draining his family's fishpond, slushing through the mud, or helping his brother Billy at the peanut warehouse. And of course, candidate Carter was seen constantly walking down the stairs from his campaign plane, with clothes bag hooked over his shoulder like an ordinary businessman.

I asked Jody Powell about the "image" that Carter projected to the public. Powell let me know that it really was the way his boss was. He said, "Of course, he's aware of the fact that it looks good on TV when he carries his own luggage. It makes him look more human. On the other hand, he doesn't throw the stuff down as soon as he enters a hotel and gets away from the cameras."

Jody Powell was Carter's confidante and press secretary for the campaign and would be in the White House after they won the election. He was also Mr. Carter's chauffeur at one time. He had certainly come a long way. At this point, they were all working very hard to get him elected. And Carter's down-to-earth sensibility was supposed to be good for votes.

"If I don't do some things for myself, I'm going to be completely helpless before we're through with this." That's how Carter explained the fact that he still took time to wash his own socks on campaign trips. And he meant it seriously. During one of the morning briefings, he asked his running mate, Walter Mondale, if he wanted a cup of coffee. When two staffers jumped up to get it, Carter waved them off. "No, no. Sit down. I'll do it," he said.

ABC's Sam Donaldson, who had fast become the dean of the Carter press corps, later said to me, "I wouldn't be surprised if Carter, as President, would climb out of Air Force One with his clothes bag over his shoulder. Carter is a very aggressive, stubborn, self-assured person." It was opinions like that that would allow the Carter administration to accuse the press of having an unfair bias against the President just four years later. His cold look alone, though, was probably enough to turn some people off. At the time, there were comparisons between Nixon's and Carter's characteristics. Sam Donaldson explained the difference to me. "Nixon was also driven to succeed," he said, "But Nixon was driven by his inferiority complex. Carter doesn't need to compensate; he's used to winning . . . He's always been in the habit of succeeding."

But his style could be off-putting, and it was especially hard for Europeans to understand how he was supposedly succeeding in the race for America's top prize, and not simply for his cold eyes. In my view, it was a matter of timing. American politicians with famous names typically earn those names in Washington, but at that time, Washington was still tainted with the stigma of the Watergate scandal. A man from Plains, Georgia, on the other hand, was outside the reach of the scandal.

Jody Powell explained much the same thing to me: "The fundamental difference between Carter and other candidates is that he was a Governor from Georgia and not a Senator from Washington." This fact made him nearly a hero in his little hometown of just 683 people—a town with one street and one private airstrip.

Only a year before, there were rarely more than two or three passersby at one time on Main Street. By the time I arrived in 1976, it was full of tourists. ("We had a hard time finding this place," they remarked.) It was also full of Carter staffers, politicians, and a horde of press people, all trying to understand the election like me. I really was living out my dream in a strange and faraway land, as I had dreamed when I was a girl. Little did I know, the strange adventure would be in America.

The people from town also saw fit to make a buck off their sudden importance and the flood of visitors. Carter had his headquarters in an old white train depot. Outside, volunteers sold everything from t-shirts to silver peanut jewelry, as well as Jimmy's autobiography they threw in free peanut recipes to boot. I also found Jimmy's mother, Miss Lillian, sitting in her old rocking chair by the door, giving autographs and dispensing advice to journalists. "Be good to Jimmy now, ya heah," she said. She made me sit next to her and keep her company.

"You have such a cute accent," she laughed.

One man even offered what he called the "Carter Country Tour." He described it as "One half hour . . . Ten miles . . . You've come this far . . . Make it an experience to remember!" Of course, he charged $2.50 for adults and $1.50 for children. His tour, which I did not go on but maybe now sounds like a good idea, took tourists to places where Jimmy lived, to his tree house, to the world's largest worm farm, and to other "never-to-be-forgotten points of interest."

A new Peanut Museum even opened beside the campaign headquarters train depot. For $1.50, tourists could buy peanuts and see anything there was to see about them. To add to this atmosphere, Carter's campaign plane had been christened "Peanut One." This was my initiation into American presidential politics.

Imagine what it looked like when a gaggle of reporters followed Jimmy on Sunday to his Southern Baptist Church, where they waited outside or even went in. Or when they stood on his farm and watched him drain his fishpond. I guess this was the behavior his people thought would win elections. He took his Southern Baptism seriously. His evangelical tendencies often got the better of him, and there was hardly a speech in which Jesus or sin didn't figure. But there was one sin that became central to his campaign at that point. It became central, as with many political injuries, because Jimmy brought it up. He would often mention the sin of adultery. He mentioned it so much that one reporter asked him, "Governor, if I was a psychiatrist, I would think there was something behind your constantly bringing up adultery." To which he followed up, "Is there?" Of course, Carter gave the reporter, to whom he usually liked to talk to, one of his icy looks.

He then added fuel to this fire with a now infamous *Playboy* interview, in which he admitted to looking "with lust at other women," and stated that his religion saved him. He was trying to change his saintly image to a more human one, but he made a fairly amusing error that was seized upon and became something of a running joke.

It also became a personal joke on my part because I had a picture taken with candidate Carter. What's funny is how Mr. Carter is looking at young, married Thea Rosenbaum in it. Once I had the picture developed, I used to show it to friends and joke, "He looks as if he has lust in his heart." And since this line had been so publicized, most people not only agreed with my depiction of the photo but also laughed.

There were really more important things going on than this talk of a lustful heart. Carter really knew his stuff when it came to international military relations, NATO, and the Warsaw Pact countries. It's also interesting in hindsight to read through my articles and see how important Cold War strategy was to the election. But despite his strong policy convictions, he was nervous about the upcoming debates. When they came, it showed, but it didn't hurt him in the polls or in people's perceptions. As Jody Powell pointed out, "Elections in this country aren't won on the issues. They're won by personalities." Carter was better at this than Ford, who, it cannot be forgotten, was Nixon's successor and pardoner.

Perhaps other presidential elections would have been more tame affairs for a German to cover. This election, however, was not. I got a first-person introduction to American politics and to the power of the homespun, and I had a lot of fun doing it.

CHAPTER 21

Inauguration

On January 20th, 1977, I was in Washington for the inauguration of Jimmy Carter. It was cold, as always. But I wasn't actually watching him take the oath with everybody else at the Capitol. Instead, I was inside the White House.

I had many connections in the Ford White House because of Vietnam. My access there was also magnified because Ford's Deputy Press Secretary was always hitting on me. It wasn't a big deal. I think he was always hitting on everyone. But it certainly helped increase the amount of time I could spend in the White House. He would invite me on official business to travel with the campaign, sit in on appointments, and the like.

As it turned out, I got inside the White House on Inauguration Day. I don't remember what business I had there, other than that I wanted to see if I could get in and learn what was going on. I never knew where I might find an interesting story.

As a last gesture, the Ford Press Office checked me into the White House. It was very strange, too, because no one was there. I almost had the place to myself. I went into the lower press office, and there wasn't a soul around. All the offices were empty. I felt like rats had fled a sinking ship.

I knew someone would have to say something to me sooner or later. I didn't belong. I thought I should at least keep looking around, if for no other reason than how interesting and strange it was to be inside the White House all by myself. It was like being backstage while a play was being performed, only you're the only one there, and you can walk around, peek out through the curtain, and even go into the dressing rooms.

To get to the Presidential Quarters, you walked from the Press Office through a set of French doors that led directly to the Colonnade. The Colonnade led directly to the East Wing. On the right was the Rose Garden. On the left was the Press Office and part of the White House. Then there was another set of French doors that also led to the East Wing and the Presidential Quarters. Through those doors were the official rooms, and of course, the private rooms were upstairs. No one had stopped me yet, so I kept exploring.

I walked right through the Colonnade and into the Presidential Quarters. I saw a lone uniformed agent as I walked. I just moved around like I belonged. I was thinking to myself, "My goodness, where did everybody go?" Then some people walked by me. By the way they looked at me, I could tell they didn't think it was strange at all that I should be standing there. A group of people walked through, carrying furniture. The doors were open, and I looked down on the South Lawn, where more furniture was waiting to go on to a truck.

They were dismantling the Ford White House. I had walked into the White House between presidencies. Suddenly, I saw Jody Powell coming through the corridor with his wife. He was showing her the White House. He must have been allowed to be there. After all, they won the election. When he saw me, he crinkled his forehead and said, "Oh, hi."

"Hey, guys. Congratulations again," I said.

He didn't say anything after that. We just looked at each other for a moment. I guess he didn't know whether I was supposed to be there, either. I know for sure this would not happen today, as I worked in the White House for many years after that, until my retirement. It's amazing that no one was paying attention, and someone could just wander through the White House at will.

I got laughs from this episode many years later, but I never wrote a story about it. This was just a moment that you laugh about, enjoy, and move on. It was also a sort of prelude to what would become my life and career, not only in the surroundings but also with whom I would work. And it did prove to me that I belonged. Jody Powell, who had only met me once in Georgia, saw me wandering the halls of the White House like a misplaced tourist, and he just assumed I belonged there. Because he assumed that, I really did belong there. I don't know the extent to which I realized it at this point, but I had come very far from Berlin and from all that had happened. My own feelings about myself may have lingered, but I had certainly done a lot to keep them at bay.

That's when I received a phone call from the Washington Bureau Chief for ARD German television. He wanted to talk about the possibility of my doing some part-time work. The industry runs on connections, and he knew that I had established quite a few American contacts in and around Washington and beyond.

When I went to see him, I wore a dress that I loved, along with a lovely, large hat that I recently had purchased. When I entered the building, there was a woman cleaning the lobby. I overheard her say, "There goes a real lady." Her comment struck me for several reasons. Most importantly, I had gotten so used to people in Vietnam saying the war was no place for a lady (and directing it at me) that I had almost gotten used to the idea of not being a lady. Of course, I also said it plenty of times as a rebuttal.

I was just a freelancer on an important job interview with an important man. I don't think I was nervous, but it certainly didn't hurt to have a complete stranger compliment me that way. There was another reason that made that moment stick with me. My parents were very attractive people. In the old pictures my father looks dashing, and my mother's beauty is striking, but I never felt that way about myself. Maybe it came from some of the things that happened to me—I don't know. I do know that I overheard my great aunt say with a perfectly straight face, "With parents as good-looking as them, what happened to her?" She meant me. I had been dragging around this notion that I was ugly ever since. If anyone told me otherwise, I just assumed they were lying.

What the cleaning woman said was certainly a very small event in the scheme of things, but it meant something to me. I walked into the Bureau Chief's office that morning with a strong sense of self.

"Darling, I have something for you," he said. "What are you doing these days?"

"I am my own boss," I said.

"Well, I need a liaison to the American networks. You can help us with the satellite feeds."

At that time, sending stories back to Germany was not always easy. You needed to go to one of the U.S. network offices and use their satellite feed. We were just a small office; we didn't have the infrastructure to have a feed of our own. Now it's different. They have a dedicated fiber line to send stories twenty-four hours a day.

"It's just a little part-time job," he said. "I know you would be perfect."

But what he described as a "little part time job" lasted about two weeks. First, I was working six hours a day, then eight hours a day and having trouble with my clients. Finally, I was working ten hours a day for ARD in Washington, and something had to give.

One of the correspondents spoke up and mentioned the fact that they were paying me part-time wages for full-time work.

I spoke with the Bureau Chief. "I'm losing all my clients. I can't keep this up. I have to be full-time."

They made me a producer. One of the best parts of the job was that they gave me a White House press pass. I actually was allowed inside now. I didn't have to sneak around on Inauguration Day.

I loved working as a producer for ARD; I spent over thirty years there. I didn't just have one or two jobs, as happens in larger companies. Because this was just a small branch that attempted to do a lot, I was able to get experience doing everything in the production of news television and more. I was able even to make documentaries and produce television spots, and early on, I became the White House Pool Producer for foreign correspondents.

It was a wonderful job that brought me in close contact with Jody Powell, but I got off to a rocky start. I learned that Jody had a bit of a temper. Shortly after I became a producer at ARD, the President was planning to make a state visit to Germany. In anticipation of this trip, I asked for an interview. Because the state visit included not only Germany but also several other European countries, the Carter White House thought it would be a good idea to do a joint interview with all the correspondents. They asked me to be the pool producer for the group of European correspondents.

The interview was supposed to happen in a few days. In preparation, I went with Jody into the Oval Office, where we would conduct the interview, to plan out how it would go. My first impression was that the room was not laid out in a way that would make it easy for all five correspondents to speak with the President.

"Where will we all sit?" I asked.

Jody pointed to the various chairs and couches.

As I began to make a suggestion, "Well, if we move the desk . . ." he cut me off.

He turned abruptly and looked at me like I was out of my mind.

"No one moves the desk of the President of the United States."

"I thought we could do anything."

"Well, that's out. You can have three people in those chairs there, and the others on the couch."

I sat on the couch. It was very soft, and you sank way down. This would make the correspondents significantly lower than the President. They would look like children seated before his throne.

"No," I said, "This won't work at all. My correspondents are not going to sit below the President."

"Take it or leave it!" he yelled and stormed out.

When he did that, I thought, "Oh my God, Thea. What are you doing? They're going to kill you for this."

I called my Bureau Chief and explained to him how Jody wanted the other correspondents to sit. I didn't think it was fair that they should be made to feel like inferiors in the way they would sit before the President.

"I won't back down on this," I told my Bureau Chief.

"I'm behind you in whatever you do, Thea." he replied.

The interview was scheduled in a few days. I didn't want to let it go. There was no need for Jody to storm out as he had. I could not let my correspondents down, nor would I allow them to be treated in that way, even inadvertently. I was determined to keep the interview.

I spent the next day sitting on the floor in front of Jody Powell's office. I said hello to the staff, and they said hello to me when I sat down. Then Jody came in and said hello to his staff and ignored me. He walked in and out of his office for the rest of the day, reading press releases and talking to various people, but never once did he even so much as look in my direction. I didn't say a word to him, either. I just sat there, which was uncomfortable for both of us considering the hallway that led to his door was tiny.

Suddenly, he threw his door open. "Thea, what do you really want?"

"We can make a compromise. We'll put a wooden board under the cushions on the couch. That way they won't sink down so low."

"Fine. Do that."

"Okay," I said, "I also need a paint sample for the walls in the Oval Office."

"Now you're starting again," he said. He looked like he was getting heated up.

"No, we're going to do this right. I need to paint the light posts the color of the walls."

He agreed.

The night before the interview, the crews were furiously working in the Oval Office to set up. Jody and I were sort of supervising, both of us making sure everyone did what was agreed upon. Suddenly, a Secret Service Agent walked in and called out, "Heads up!"

I was so involved in what I was doing that I hadn't heard him. Jody Powell grabbed me by the arm and whispered, "Stand back. POTUS [President of the United States] is coming in."

When I looked up, there was Jimmy Carter, in jeans and a cowboy shirt, with a lady friend entering the Oval Office. He proudly showed her everything and ignored us.

All I could think was, "I hope he doesn't hang out too long. We've got to get finished with the setup!"

Then the President nonchalantly waved good-bye and hustled his visitor back to the East Wing.

From that day on, whenever we had multiple foreign correspondents, I was the pool producer.

CHAPTER 22

Camp David

As soon as President Carter was in office, he started traveling with a vengeance. Four or five countries and two continents were not unheard of in one trip. But probably Carter's greatest accomplishment was the Camp David Accords. They were hashed out in Maryland, where the Presidential retreat is, but when the deal between Israeli Prime Minister Menachim Begin and Egypt's President Anwar Sadat was in jeopardy, we suddenly had to fly to the Middle East. Since this trip came without warning, we had almost no time to get ready. We even had our vaccinations arranged by Jody Powell at the White House. Otherwise, we would never have been able to travel on such short notice.

Even though the trip was arranged so quickly and was taken under serious auspices, we enjoyed ourselves. Some people in the Press Corps and in the White House probably enjoyed themselves too much on these excursions. On a trip to Panama, as I was leaving the hotel to deliver my story, I saw Chief of Staff Hamilton Jordan taking the elevator down to the lobby with a brunette on his arm, looking a bit drunk. When I returned, Ham was riding up from the bar with a blonde on his arm. This time, the girl looked like she was practically holding him up.

That was the way it was. Later, on our trip to Cairo, I got on to one of the press planes, which we called the "Zoo Plane," to leave the country. The stewardess handed me a bottle of Champagne and asked how many glasses I needed. It's not like that anymore. It's much more serious now. People are too busy. We were able to have a lot more fun then. In 1978, we traveled with the President practically around the globe and had a great time. One trip began in Caracas, Venezuela, and then went to Rio de Janeiro before going to Lagos, Nigeria. From Lagos we were to travel on to Monrovia, Liberia.

By the time we hit Nigeria, we were all beginning to get tired and were getting a little wild. On the last evening, after we had already taken our film to the airport, we were having drinks at the hotel. A few people were still working, especially the American press. The atmosphere was relaxed enough that I challenged Jody to an underwater swimming contest in the pool, which Jody lost.

As it got later, we all stayed around the pool deck. Sam Donaldson suddenly walked inside the pool restaurant and sat on a bench with his back to the window. Everyone could see him from the pool deck. This included Jody, some White House staffers, correspondents, Hodding Carter from the State Department, and some off-duty Secret Service guys.

That's when Jody got an idea. It was around midnight. He suggested, "Let's get Donaldson. It's time. He needs to go swimming, too."

So we went and got a few Secret Service Agents. These guys were pretty strong.

I was wearing a bikini from the pool and still dripping wet. I wrapped a towel around me and we marched all together into the restaurant and up to Sam. Of course, Jody stood behind us. He wasn't going to have anything to do with it. He was a little chicken shit when it came to stuff like that, but he started it all.

I sat next to Donaldson on the bench with everybody else standing around the table, staring at him. I said, "Hi Sam. How are things? We think you've worked long enough." He just looked up. Then I said, "You know, Sam, if I were you, I would take my wallet out of my pocket and leave it on the table. How heavy are your shoes, by the way? You may want to take them off as well."

"Woman," he said, "what do you have in mind? Now stop it."

"Now, Sam, just let it happen."

Then the guys, without saying a word, picked up the table in front of Sam and put it to the side. Jody was grinning from ear to ear. The agents grabbed Donaldson and raised him up over their heads and walked out toward the pool deck. Sam just folded his hands over his chest, so he looked like a body being carried overhead while I was walking next to them.

I looked up at him. They were holding him well above their heads. I said, "Do you have anything else in your pockets you might want to get rid of? Maybe your credentials?"

Of course, the Africans were looking at us like, "These Americans are completely nuts."

We marched him to the pool. Donaldson was shouting down to me, "Every condemned man gets a last word. Every condemned man gets a last word."

I looked at Jody, and he agreed, saying, "Oh, come on, he's right. Let him down to have a last word."

So they let him down, and, without hesitating, Sam turned and jumped into the pool with his clothes on. When that happened, Jody said, "That Donaldson, he did it again." He wasn't happy that Sam Donaldson had gotten the better of him again and had jumped in more or less on his own. Of course, he still had all his clothes on.

Later, a bunch of us wound up in Jody's Presidential Suite. (The President always stayed in a separate hotel.) Jody always loved to sing Southern songs from his childhood. There was a grand piano in the suite. Jody kept saying to me, "Come on. You've had piano lessons. Why don't you play something?"

"No, I don't play the stuff you're singing. I'm not going to do it," I said.

We ended up sitting on the floor, drinking gin and tonics and singing Georgia songs until very early in the morning. Then we went to our rooms, took a shower, and got on the plane for Monrovia, Liberia.

Just about everybody walking off the plane in Monrovia was in bad shape. It was so hot, and we hadn't gotten any sleep. The heat got to people. We were dropping like flies, including me. Two people had to grab me on each side coming out of the plane so that I didn't fall down.

Later, the Press Corps and White House staffers were at the port waiting for President Carter to arrive with President Tolbert of Liberia. We had been there some time when someone in the Press Corps shouted, "Hey, there's a body down there!" We turned to look into the water, and sure enough, there was a body floating in the harbor. It had a rope around its neck that was tied to one of the docks. We told nearby people about the floating man, but nobody came to do anything about it. We just went on with the event. "Well, this is Africa," we thought. I suppose they weren't going to come and fish out the body while the two presidents were there.

Our travels with the President always seemed to be like that. The press was not allowed anywhere near the retreat at Camp David, except for a little place where we could snap pictures of the dignitaries as they walked off the helicopter. But that was all. The press were kept outside the camp in the American Legion Hall in a town called Thurmont, Maryland. We had briefings there every day. At the briefings, they told us nothing. The whole time we were there, we only heard rumors of how the talks were breaking down and how either Israel or Egypt was getting ready to walk away from the table. Sadat and Begin wouldn't even talk to each other, unless, of course, Carter forced them. The Israelis tried to leak that things looked bad, but nobody really knew anything.

This lasted thirteen days. Every morning we drove 90 miles from Washington to the little town of Thurmont in the Catoctin Mountains. On Sunday, September 17th, 1978, Carter secured an agreement for a peace treaty. The White House wanted to make the best of this agreement. In the late afternoon, they called us into the Legion Hall, where they told us that they had a framework for a peace treaty and that the signing of this was to be held at the White House in ninety minutes. "We'll try to wait for everybody," they told us.

Everyone made a mad dash to their cars. We got out of that little town as fast as we could. On the highway, we hit speeds of 90 to 100 miles per hour so we could report on the signing in the East Room. I don't know if someone called ahead or not, but no one was pulled over for driving like a maniac. There were a lot of cars racing to D.C. that evening.

The fact that they had managed to sign the Accords—a framework for peace—was actually very moving. Even the White House Press Corps was moved by the event. Finally, there would be peace between Egypt and Israel.

It wasn't long after that little ceremony that the Accords were on their way down the drain. Within a few months, it didn't look like there was going to be a peace treaty after all. Carter was determined to make it happen, however. He decided to go to Cairo and Jerusalem and make an effort to finish the peace deal. He announced that he was going to make this trip on March 7th, 1979. The news came on March 2nd, which gave us no time to plan. We typically had weeks to plan for trips—now we just had days. This was unheard of until then. Presidents don't just pick up and leave. They don't do that because they are responsible to the public and have the press to worry about. They also have to send in an advance team to make sure it's safe.

"If you're coming, I need to know by this afternoon. Vaccines will be given here," Jody said.

I got our crew together as fast as I could. We went in for the vaccinations, and in five days we were in Cairo. We were ready for another foreign adventure. Even the importance of the event didn't slow us down from enjoying ourselves.

The worst part of the trip was that we got absolutely no information to report on from the Carter people. Carter wanted to do everything without the press, and that may have been a good idea. But as a journalist, I couldn't stand not having any news. The White House people just gave me a blank stare whenever I asked for information. I went to one of the deputy press secretaries and started to cry. "You can't do this to us. We have to have some pictures, at least."

He was so impressed by the fact that I was crying that he made a phone call and organized some buses for us. They took us to a hotel garden. In the background stood the Pyramids. Sadat and Carter made statements, and we were able to get pictures. It was better than nothing.

From Cairo we went to Jerusalem on March 10th. As soon as we arrived, we heard that Begin wasn't going to do it. Rumors were flying that things were not going well with Begin. Finally, on the evening of March 12th, Jody briefed the White House Press. I was sitting in the back of the room on top of a table, a telephone at my ear. I was calling my home office in Hamburg and giving a running report.

Just to look at Jody, you knew that it was not going well; it was going to be a complete failure. We thought that Begin had squashed the deal. And now we were traveling back to Cairo, we assumed, just so Carter could relay to Sadat what Begin had said and end this thing.

On the phone with Hamburg, I said, "Look, I know nothing is going to come of this, but just to be sure, please order me a satellite from Cairo tomorrow."

"Okay, are you sure?"

"Yeah, I'm sure. I don't know why, but I'm sure."

It was midnight. That night was also Donaldson's birthday, and some people had gone to a party for him, including Jody.

In the morning, we left for Cairo. The flight took less than an hour, so we were there in no time and expected to return to the States quickly. In Cairo, we didn't even go back to town. That's how little even the White House thought of this trip. We just waited on the tarmac while Carter met with Sadat in a private hanger.

At that time, we had two press planes. One was the "Zoo Plane," which was a Pan Am jet. All the television crews were on it. The other was a TWA plane, which was the writers' plane and had mostly newspaper guys. We had to wait out on the tarmac because we were only supposed to be there a short time. But as it took longer, the TV crews went to the TWA plane and started to party. Things got really wild on that parked plane. They were having fun with the stewardesses in the back until the Purser came and threw them all out.

"I'm going to have to get somebody in here to clean this all up. You made a mess," he said.

So now we all were waiting out on the tarmac together. But as the hours passed, it began to dawn on us that if it was taking this long, then maybe something was happening. If all Carter came to do was deliver the bad news, then we would have left already. Suddenly, we saw Jody come out. He called over the late Helen Thomas, who was working at UPI; the AP guy; and my husband, who was a radio pool producer. I ran up and asked him, "What's going on?"

"They obviously have something, and they want to announce it."

Finally, Sadat and Carter came out, and Sadat said, "I agree with everything Begin said. We have a peace treaty."

You knew immediately that this was a historic moment. The problem now was that we had to get the news out. The White House arranged some buses to take us back to the Hilton. Everyone was excited to get back and scrambled out of the buses and over hedges just to get inside the hotel and find a working telephone line. There were no landlines out of the Hilton at that time, just the telephone lines the White House had installed. Egypt had very few phone lines at all.

I told my boss Peter Merseburger: "Run as fast as you can to Cairo TV right now. I set up a live feed for the 'Tagesschau' [our evening news]. I'll get through to our office somehow." But that was easier said than done.

In the lobby, I found a telephone that only worked inside the hotel. When I picked it up, I identified myself as "White House" and asked for Signal Corps, which handled the communications for the White House. To my great surprise, the hotel operator said, "Okay," and patched me through to them. When they picked up, I said, "I need a line into town."

"All right, what's the number?"

I gave them the number, and they patched me through. The phone rang. Then I heard in German, "Hello, this is ARD German Television, Cairo."

"I can't believe it. This actually worked. I'm at the Hilton. This is Thea. Peter is on his way. We have a peace treaty. Sadat and Carter just announced it at the airport. Please go find Peter and help him get to the studio."

We went live with the story for the "Tagesschau." One of the best moves I ever made was deciding to order that satellite feed from Jerusalem.

On the return flight on the "Zoo Plane," my friend, who was a stewardess, gave me champagne. I can't remember all the things that happened on the return flight, however, I'm sure it involved drinking and singing songs from Georgia with Jody. We also heard complaining from some correspondents because they didn't get advance word the night before. All this, of course, was followed by a lot of sleeping. We all were absolutely exhausted.

CHAPTER 23

Reagan

Reagan stood at Check Point Charlie in West Berlin. It was June 12, 1987. He was there for the 750th anniversary of Berlin. We all watched as he placed his foot over the line marking the East/West divide, almost like a mischievous kid.

"Am I in East Germany now? Am I in East Germany now?"

"Yes. You theoretically are in East Germany."

He had come to survey the border between East and West and to make a speech. Of course, I came along with the American press, but this was not the first time I had traveled back to Germany with the American news media. This time around, I had decided not to brag about my home city.

When we came with the Carter administration a few years prior, it was a different story. I bragged a lot about Berlin then, but I was disappointed. We landed at Tempelhof Airport, which is where the chocolate bomber flew after World War II and delivered Hershey's bars by parachute to me and many other children.

It was a homecoming for me in many ways. Beyond the history of the postwar period, I told everyone with whom I was traveling, including Jody Powell, how lovely Berlin was. I was just bursting with pride for this great and beautiful city.

From the airport we drove to the Ku'damm, which was the main avenue for West Berlin and was famous at the time and still is. We were all together on a group of buses headed for an event after landing.

This was the first time everyone would see the city from the ground. I had just finished telling them how lovely it was here. But looking out the bus window, I thought, "Shit, Thea, this is terrible." The buildings were so grey and depressing and dreary. They still had the look of World War II. They even still wore the dust and soot from that time. The city as it is now is very different. The buildings have since been washed and painted, but at the time, this was still the Cold War. It was a dark city.

I hadn't been back to Berlin in several years at that point, and the city was better in my memory and imagination than it was in real life. Of course, I felt very embarrassed for telling all these people how wonderful my city was. If they had listened to me, they would have been expecting a northern Paris. So when I traveled with Reagan, I made sure to keep quiet about my home city altogether. I would let them find out for themselves what it was like, and maybe the charm would win them over even if their expectations were not overblown.

By the time we got to the Brandenburg Gate with President Reagan, I was hardly thinking about what the city looked like. Berlin was divided in half by a terrible wall, and the Brandenburg Gate sat between East and West in "no man's land." This was a very public and ugly scar on the city's face that Reagan had come to point out and to make a point about. Bragging about the beauty of the city certainly would serve little purpose.

All the press were assembled, along with mobs of people, to watch the President. Reagan was a Cold War Warrior, after all, and had been known as one for decades, but the speech he was about to make before that Wall would become iconic beyond anything he had done before.

Before the Brandenburg Gate, Reagan stood and delivered his famous line: "Mr. Gorbachev, open this gate! Mr. Gorbachev, tear down this wall!"

When he said that, I thought to myself, "Not in our lifetime, pal," not knowing that one day it would really be true. I thought it was lip service that didn't mean a thing. The Soviets would never take the wall down—they couldn't afford it—and everybody in the East would run over to the free side if that happened. Now that I had become Americanized and took such infrequent trips back to my home city, I had a new understanding of the city's divide. It was obviously divided, and the people there felt it bitterly. But leaving and returning made me feel how profound the split really was. I thought it was never going to change. Decades before, I had seen President Kennedy showing his solidarity with Berliners while delivering another iconic speech. But what had it meant? It had meant so much at the time, but in the end, what did it really mean? Besides being a wonderful photo opportunity for young Kennedy, nothing came of it.

I know Reagan meant what he said; I just didn't think it was possible. Of course, we had no idea how much trouble the USSR was actually in and that they were on the verge of coming apart. Reagan was using this trip as a campaign against the Soviets since there was no longer anything for him to campaign for back home. The way Reagan was treating the trip was both serious, as in his speech, and funny, as when he put his foot over the line. He was always like that. His attitude, in this respect, conveyed the truth about the Wall: that it was absurd. It was also deadly serious because the East Germans would not play with people crossing the border. Reagan's attitude was that of a sober man with a sense of humor. It's interesting that this man would bring the great Soviet empire to the brink of collapse by calling their bluff, in effect. They could not compete economically with the West, and he knew it.

I had known Reagan since his presidential campaign in 1980. I sat on the campaign bus across the aisle from him and his wife Nancy. He was holding a single red rose in his hand that someone had given to him on the campaign stop. It was obvious he didn't know what to do with it. He didn't want to hold it, and he wasn't going to get off the next stop with it in his hand.

He turned to Nancy and gave it to her. It was Valentine's Day, after all. His gesture simply may have been in the spirit of the day. But she obviously didn't want the rose, either. It seemed by her face that she was thinking, "What am I going to do with that?"

Suddenly, he turned around and handed it to me. "Happy Valentine's Day," he said.

"Thank you," I replied, and he sat back down next to Nancy. Of course, I was thinking that I didn't want the rose, either. We were working. I didn't need anything more to carry. I didn't know where to put it, but I wasn't going to say that to Reagan.

It was just a few weeks later that we were in Nashua, New Hampshire, for Reagan's primary debate with George H.W. Bush. *The*

Nashua Telegraph was supposed to be sponsoring the event, but the Federal Election Committee ruled that the paper had to withdraw its support. The *Telegraph* was not allowed to sponsor the event if it only was going to be between Bush and Reagan, which it was. In the light of this ruling, Reagan decided to pay for the debate himself. He also wanted to include the other candidates, who were still vying for the Republican nomination.

When we arrived at the gymnasium, there was some confusion. Reagan thought that all the candidates were going to be included in the debate now that he was footing the bill. But the *Telegraph* had only set up space for Reagan and Bush on stage. The moderator was the *Telegraph* editor John Breen. Reagan and Breen began arguing. They were right next to each other at a table on stage. Then Breen suddenly said, "Would the sound man please turn Mr. Reagan's mike off?"

Reagan stood immediately. He was visibly angered. This was the first time that we had ever seen him angry on the campaign. He picked up the microphone stand from the table. The people in the auditorium were making noise. He asked, "Is this on?" Someone shouted, "Yes." Then he sat back down and began to talk. Breen again said, "Would you turn his microphone off, please?"

That's when Reagan got really angry. "I am paying for this microphone, Mr. Green." People cheered that comment. They were going wild in the gymnasium.

I was with the press, and we were all laughing. All the candidates came in after that and were able to make one statement. No one seemed to care that Reagan had called the moderator Mr. Green when his name was Breen. It didn't matter, after all. That line of his went into the history books. And he was right: he really was paying for that microphone. That was on February 23, 1980. He certainly had shown he had a backbone. He completely shut down the moderator and was glaring at him. We all knew he could blow his top.

He could also be funny, as he later showed at Check Point Charlie. Whenever his campaign plane took off, someone would always roll an orange up the aisle to Reagan, and he would always roll it back. We generally didn't follow the rules people made on commercial flights; campaign planes and especially the press planes were much looser, to say the least. But on one occasion when the orange rolled up the aisle, Reagan threw it back. The only problem was that he hit a producer from CBS right in the eye. He felt so bad. He came running down the aisle and apologized: "I hope I didn't give you a concussion." She was fine.

I continued following candidate Reagan around New Hampshire, but the trail ran cold in a place called Berlin in a moment that, to me, wasn't funny at all.

We were in the middle of absolutely nowhere at a tiny airport. This was in the northern part of the state in the White Mountains. From here the campaign was heading over to Vermont for a quick stop, but Reagan's people waited until the last moment to tell us we couldn't go along with them.

"There's not enough room on this trip, so we're not taking foreigners."

I was furious.

I already had my correspondent Peter flying into that airport. And since it was such a small strip, there were no commercial flights. He was flying in on a two-seater. There was no way I could leave with the rest of my crew on such a small plane, so we were stranded there.

There were still a few of Reagan's people around. I started yelling at a Reagan official. I didn't know his name at the time.

"You have some nerve leaving us stranded here. What am I going to do with this crew? How am I going to catch up? They don't even have taxis or rental cars here. And my boss is coming in on a tiny plane, so we can't even fly out on that."

"I'm sorry. I'm sorry," he said.

He spoke a little German, but I didn't care to listen to him. He just said, "Catch our campaign bus, and we'll meet up."

So we waited for Reagan's bloody campaign bus. When it came, we were the only people riding on it. On the way through New Hampshire, we had to stop and wash the bus. We decided that if we were going to ride on it alone, we might as well stop at a liquor store, too. We arrived a little happier at the next stop.

After Reagan was elected, I was looking to do an interview with his new National Security Advisor, Richard Allen. Journalists always ask for this kind of interview. You rarely get them, so I was surprised when Richard agreed to speak with me since I only represented a German television network. The first thing he said to me in his office was, "You have your boots on, but where is your whip?"

"What?"

"Well, you sure looked like you were going to whip me when you yelled at me in the airport in Berlin, New Hampshire."

"Oh my God. That was you." I was so angry at the time that I didn't remember who it was.

"You know," he continued, "It's because I remembered you that you are getting the interview."

He thought it was funny. When I relayed this conversation to my boss, he said, "Well, good thing he thought it was funny."

Allen wasn't the only member of the Reagan administration that I knew. I was fairly close with Reagan's Press Secretary, Jim Brady, as well. I first met him when he held the same position for another candidate. I was looking to do a piece on the President, so I tried to use that connection. I went to the White House and met with Brady. I told him what I was looking for. "We would like to do a long, 45-minute documentary on the President. A day in the life of the President. Can you help us?"

"Yeah, I can, but you and a thousand others want to do this."

It was just the beginning of Reagan's term. "That's why we want to start early," I said.

He told me to go to a fundraising event and try to make contact there. This wasn't what I was looking for since anyone in the press could get this kind of access. I wanted to be close to the President. Then he told me, "Go over to the Hilton and wait in the press bin. See if you can meet him and maybe walk out with him."

This kind of access wasn't going to get me anywhere, either. Instead, I rushed over to our office and arranged to have lunch with a friend who was visiting from our German home office. I told him about the Reagan documentary I was trying to develop. "But I don't know what kind of access I can get."

Suddenly, we got word that something had happened at the Hilton. This was before cell phones, so rumors passed from person to person, sometimes very quickly. I rushed back to the Press Office. We had no official word on what was going on.

Then it came in. "Shots fired at the Hilton." And then: "We think Jim Brady is lying on the ground, dead."

I rushed to the White House. When I arrived, no one knew what was going on there, either. The place was in chaos. Then we heard that the President had been shot, too, and was at Washington Hospital.

When John Hinckley shot the President, a Secret Service Agent immediately tackled Reagan into the limo. The door was open, and they both fell inside. The agent was lying on top of Reagan. As the limo pulled away, Reagan said, "Get off me, you son-of-a-bitch. You broke a rib." The agent looked down and saw that the President had blood on his lips. At that point, he immediately rerouted the limo to the hospital. There, Reagan insisted on walking in on his own, but he was having trouble at that point. They really had to help him inside.

Apparently Reagan didn't feel the bullet enter his body because the Secret Service Agent hit him hard at the same time as the bullet struck. Reagan thought the agent injured him.

Jim Brady was really hurt. He was shot in the head. It took him a long time to recuperate. He didn't even recognize me when I saw him some time later. It was very sad. Jim was such a good guy. It's almost more difficult to lose friends in acts of violence during a time of peace than it is during war. At least in a war, injuries and death are part of the program. You don't expect someone you know to be shot in the head leaving a fundraiser.

War seemed to be all around me. And in America, in the '80s, where prosperity was supposed to reign, political violence and aggression were prevalent. Somehow the human condition seemed to bring about these kinds of encounters. I covered Klan rallies in Chicago, where we had to run and hide from the barrage of stones people threw at the marching members. I covered a coal miner's strike in West Virginia, which felt like a low-level conflict; the L.A. riots; and natural disasters like the San Francisco earthquake. The later half of the 20th century was supposed to be less violent than other times, but these were major crises. I had seen so much of disaster, both man-made and natural, since I was a girl that it appeared to me more the norm than health and peace.

As the producer for ARD German Television here in the States, I was the one who organized and transmitted so many of these stories. It was my job and my life. I was in charge, and that was a problem for my marriage. I think Dick wanted me to look up to him, as I had always done, but I just couldn't. I had changed. I was more confident in myself. And we grew apart. We were no longer in the same relationship. It just couldn't work anymore, so we separated.

We would still talk. We were still friends. Dick would still give me a heads-up on news stories he knew of. During elections, he would let me know early which way his network was calling the election. He even called me to let me know that David was dying.

David had learned more than a year earlier that he had terminal cancer. The doctor told him that he probably had two years to live but only one good year left. Hearing this, David decided to keep his illness a secret for his last good year before the sickness took real hold. I think I would have killed him if he had done that to me. But it worked for them. When the year was up, he began to feel sick, and he told Martha what was happening. Then they held on to the news until their son Adam graduated from college. Their daughter had already graduated. When Adam was finished, they told the family. That's when Dick learned and called me.

David died in November of 1993. He was able to plan his funeral down to the letter. He was only fifty years old.

CHAPTER 24

The Wall

My husband Jens and I were standing at the bottom of the staircase to the apartment above George H.W. Bush's Library in College Station, Texas, when we saw the former President and Barbara Bush walking down toward us. We were here for an event in the late nineties, before his son became President. Jens was a freelance cameraman for ARD German Television. I met him when he was a full-time cameraman with the company. Cameramen worked for ARD in the States on five-year rotations. This meant they went back to Germany after their time was up. When Jens's five years were up, he didn't want to go. I was divorced from Dick at that point. Jens told me that he was madly in love with me and that he wouldn't go back to Germany.

"But you have to go back," I said, "Don't be silly."

In fact, he didn't have to go back. He quit ARD rather than return to Germany and founded his own company as a cameraman. We were married several years later.

As he was filming Bush coming up the wide staircase, Bush started waving at me and stopped to shake my hand, "How are you?"

Jens whispered, "Oh great, Thea, you ruined my shot."

Bush was very gracious. He had always been very kind to me and equally kind to other journalists while he was in office. I never heard a bad word about him in this respect. I certainly never complained about the way he treated me. He really was a good man. Outside of his graciousness, which came into play on the international stage, the events that happened on his watch were tremendous. He had been a diplomat earlier in his career, and he knew how to operate on a world stage. The events he oversaw and influenced as President impacted my life, though I never would have seen it coming.

It was early November, 1989. Bush had been President for a little less than a year. He had defeated Michael Dukakis of Massachusetts to take up the Reagan mantle, and now he was in power. He seemed well-suited to the tasks at hand.

My husband and I were at New York's John F. Kennedy International Airport getting ready to fly to Bonn, Germany. We were headed there for my parent's 50th wedding anniversary. We were delayed, so we were standing around at the gate, just waiting. At that point, I noticed Tom Brokaw, anchorman for NBC News, also waiting for the same flight. He said hello as he saw me approach. I asked him why he was going to Germany. Brokaw told me that they were going to do their show live from Berlin. There were a lot of demonstrations at that time in East Germany. It seemed as if the state of things was getting out of hand and that something might be ready to burst. Brokaw went on to say, "We thought it would be interesting to set up in front of the Brandenburg Gate and do the evening news right from there."

"That sounds like a plan. I think you're going at the right time." I could never have known how right the time actually would be.

The next evening, I was sitting with my father in our apartment in Bonn. We were watching the nightly news, which in Germany comes on at 8:00 p.m. rather than at 6:00, as in the U.S. It was November the 9th, 1989. The news showed an East Berlin press conference. There was an East German speaker who said something to the effect: "All East Germans will be issued passports so that they can travel."

This was unheard of for the people in the East at the time. A reporter stood up and asked, "Do you know when this will take effect?" The speaker turned and mumbled to someone behind the podium. Then he turned back and said, "As far as we know, it takes effect immediately."

My father and I looked at each other. Then he said, "Did you just hear what that guy said?"

"No, he didn't say that," I replied.

"No, he didn't say that," my father agreed.

"I think he said that."

We just couldn't believe that it was all over so quickly and easily, and in such an offhand way as this press conference. East Germany had opened its borders to immigration and travel. As important as the Wall had been, you would expect to find out through some high decree to the sound of trumpets. But this felt like almost accidental news: no fanfare.

That evening, the East Berliners were the first to come out. It was an unbelievable night. We watched on ARD News as the first East German walked over the border, a little cautious, as if he were walking in total darkness. He didn't know if he might walk into a wall or a door or, in this case, a bullet. After the first person crossed, others followed him. They must have seen the same news conference as we had. Behind the border crossing on the East Berlin side, you could see thousands of people assembling and yelling to open the Gate. The border guards didn't know what to do—it was all so sudden. But they finally just gave up and opened the barrier. People walked and ran and pushed their way to the West, greeted by hundreds of West Berliners with champagne. But the first thing that many of these people requested wasn't beer or champagne, but bananas. The next day, West Berliners bought up all the bananas in the city and handed them to the Easterners as they crossed.

People even climbed up on top of the wall, which had been such a dominant presence for so many years. It had cut through neighborhoods and divided friends and families. It was absurd, after all, but it was reality. As they stood atop the Wall, it became apparent that this was real, and also how small and silly the Wall had been.

Everyone has seen the images of people on the Wall greeting each other after so many years. Many of the best images and pieces of footage came from Tom Brokaw's newscast. He had the only crew reporting live in front of the Wall when it all started happening, including the German networks. He wasn't just there first; he was there before it all began. He was very lucky. It just so happened that he was giving his evening news live from the Brandenburg Gate. Brokaw always said that he couldn't believe how fortunate he was. "Talk about being at the right place at the right time."

I never thought I would see the Wall fall in my lifetime, but I did. And I was there to see it happen since I was in Germany. I wasn't in Berlin but in Bonn with my family, watching a piece of history that directly involved us. It was a fitting end to the Cold War. We were very happy, of course, that this was happening. We couldn't believe it. There had been no indication that the Wall would fall or that suddenly the Easterners would be allowed to travel outside their country. Of course, something had been brewing for quite some time. There had been the regular Monday demonstrations and thousands of refugees coming to the West through Eastern Block countries. But to me, the Wall was an irreversible fact and would remain indelible.

There was no telling what would happen next with Germany—whether it would be reunified or another option. But in the opening hours and days, it didn't matter what happened in the future. With the overall political situation, what mattered was that the Germans were reconnected with one another once again. It was President George Bush who had worked toward this event both under Reagan and during his own presidency. He later told us in an interview that when he heard through a translator that Gorbachev did not mind if the Germans reunited if only they could handle it, Bush actually asked for a retranslation. He thought it was a mistake.

The Wall fell, and everyone was uncertain what would happen next. This was a great moment of victory for the West, but President Bush didn't take a victory lap. Doing so may have incited the Russian military. Even Gorbachev was pleased with Bush's grace in victory and in the face of an enemy's misfortune and unwinding. And it was a victory; there is no doubt about that.

As soon as we could, we visited my family's house in Kleinmachnow. We couldn't go right away because they still had to take down the Wall. We had kept the title to the house for all those years; my grandmother insisted on it. For our title, we received an inconsequential amount of rent from the people who lived there. This was paid in East German Marks that were worth virtually nothing. For any repairs on the house, we had to pay in West German Marks, which were obviously worth more than the repairs would have cost in East German money. Now, after all these years, we could return. We hadn't been allowed to go there unless we had immediate family living in the house. Otherwise, we couldn't get the papers necessary to travel to Kleinmachnow, which was very close to Berlin. The trip before the Wall fell would have taken a day and a half. Now, it was just a five-minute drive away.

We drove down the road toward the house. I could remember this place so vividly, and all that happened here. I remembered walking down these very streets with my mother as we emerged from a Berlin that would never be the same. As we passed the neighbors' house now, I could picture the soldiers who had tried to hurt my mother in the basement. And further, I could see myself as a child walking hand-in-hand from the train station with my grandfather.

We arrived at the cottage. It was so much smaller than I remembered it. It was like a shack compared to the large home I had in my memory. But the house was real and in front of me after all these years of separation. The only part that remained true to my memory was the garden in back. The house was the same, but it was just smaller than I remembered. The East Germans had done nothing by way of renovations. It was as if they had preserved it in a time capsule from the immediate postwar period, and now it was ours again with all the baggage that came with it.

My father didn't want to keep the house. He didn't have anything against the house or a reason to get rid of it other than the fact that the market was extremely volatile following the fall of the Wall and Germany's reunification. When he saw the real estate market was high and the price we could get for the house was good, he sold. My cousins objected. My uncle thought the market would only go higher. Only a year or so later real estate prices crashed, and my father looked very smart.

It was also at about this time, when the West was in such ascendancy and triumph, that I was shocked by something I encountered in the United States. I had done several stories in the past on the Ku Klux Klan. They took my last name, Rosenbaum, to be German and allowed me access on several occasions. I always took advantage of it because it made for a good story. I had met with David Duke and had been to various rallies around the country. But on this occasion, my film crew and I traveled to do a story on the Klan in Alabama.

What I found in Alabama was really scary. The Grand Wizard (an absurd title if ever there was one) promised to give me an interview.

This was a weapons show for the Ku Klux Klan. It was held in a clearing in the woods in the middle of nowhere. They had everything from handguns to machine guns there. They were selling these weapons. In the middle of that show was an old school bus. The KKK just seemed to me like an oddity of American culture or the vestige of a once powerful and dangerous organization. They were a curiosity to me, and one that was slightly amusing. It's not that I didn't know their history and their violence; it was that they were rather silly by this point. Except at this rally, I realized how serious they were.

The gathering had something to do with protesting busing, and in that spirit the main event was the burning of a bus in the middle of a field. But before that could happen, we heard gunshots. We rushed over to the spot with our cameras rolling to see what happened. When we arrived, we saw that several clansmen had caught two black men. Now a group of white men were actually holding them prisoner because they were black.

These men were apparently just walking near the field, and a few KKK members had gotten hold of them. They were now discussing what they should do with them. I didn't know if they would kill them or what they would do. This was modern America, and here they were contemplating what I feared was a lynching.

"Let them go," I said. I then turned to my cameraman at the time and told him, "Just keep rolling, whatever you do. They won't hurt us if you just keep filming."

"Turn that camera off," someone said, and people began pushing at the camera.

"Don't turn the camera off. Just let those men go. We won't turn the camera off. They have done nothing. They were just walking by," I said.

"They were spying on us."

"They weren't spying on you." I remained adamant in this crowd of clansmen, who were dressed in regular clothing. Later, they were going to put on their costumes for the bus burning. All of a sudden, they let the two black men go. The two were obviously frightened. It was getting dark by that point, and someone suddenly set the bus on fire. We moved in that direction to capture the blaze on film. That's when shots were fired behind us, very close. Everyone near us hit the ground. The shooting continued. We couldn't tell who was shooting or why.

Were they drunk people, just happy to shoot their guns in the air, or was it something worse?

While we lay on the ground, the fire from the bus ignited the grass, and we suddenly had to make a choice. We could either lay where we were, and let the fire get us, or move backwards toward the shooting.

"I'll be damned if I'm going to get burned or shot in the back in this place," I said, and we started to move toward the shots. The shooting ceased.

As absurd as it sounds, it was more absurd in person, yet it was really happening. This wasn't Honduras or Vietnam or some other war zone. This was America.

CHAPTER 25

Honduras to Vietnam

My Bureau Chief Fritz Pleitgen and I stood outside a military camp in Honduras with our TV crew. The Iran Contra Affair had recently broken, and we were investigating the training camps there. The heart of the scandal was that senior Reagan administration officials had been accused of selling weapons to Iran and using the proceeds to finance a counter-revolutionary group known as the Contras against the Communist Sandinista government in Nicaragua.

We had flown to Honduras, where the Contras were headquartered, to see if we could get into one of these camps. We were in the capital of the country, Tegucigalpa. Fritz was having me produce the story, so I had traveled there ahead of him, which was often the case. When he arrived, I informed him that we might have a confrontation with the police, the military, or the Americans. Since I had been here, I learned that there was quite a bit of hostility toward the press in this story.

"I'll be the bad guy and demand cooperation," I said. And he would be the nice guy who pleaded for cooperation. You'd be surprised how often this "good cop/bad cop" routine works. Before Fritz arrived, I had already secured a guide in the capital who said that he could take me to one of the Contras' training camps, where there were Americans. This last point was the story itself. Americans training rebels to fight against the Communist government was big news, especially when coupled with arms sales to Iran for financing.

We left the hotel with our guide and headed into the surrounding mountains. It was later in the evening, just verging on dusk, when we arrived at the camp. There was little more here than a tent city. Suddenly Contra soldiers walked up to us threateningly. They were excited and angry that we were there. They had their rifles drawn and were pointing them at me.

Fritz said, "This is iffy, Thea. We could disappear out here."

The good cop/bad cop routine was probably not going to carry any weight here. I told the soldiers that we were reporting on a story, and we just wanted some footage. Whether they fully understood me or not, I couldn't be sure. They were waving their guns, shouting back to the tents in the compound, and barking commands at us. An American officer then came running out with his own rifle drawn. He also seemed upset. At least I could understand him. Fritz and I just looked at each other. But as the American officer got closer, he slowed and said, "Thea?"

"Yes."

"My God, is that you? I haven't seen you since Vietnam. How are you?"

I couldn't remember how I knew this American officer, but it was a good thing that I did. "I'm very good. How have you been? We were just doing a story on the Contras. Would it be okay if we filmed the compound?"

"Oh yeah, sure. It's fine."

And then he commanded his men to get out of their tents and do a few drills for us. The officer wanted us to see how disciplined the men were. The soldiers poured out of their barracks and fell in line. I felt bad because it seemed they had already turned in for the night. Now they had to drill for us. However, we got some great footage of the Contras. Fritz couldn't believe our luck. It was amazing to him that I happened to know somebody from Vietnam who was now training guerilla fighters in the jungles of Honduras.

He even recalled the story many years later, in 2007, at my retirement party. It got a big reception then. I knew all those years before that if you wanted to be anybody in journalism you had to go to Vietnam. I just didn't realize how long a shadow Vietnam and my time there would cast over my career, and how much help it would actually give me.

Vietnam wasn't just a boost to my career. It had remained with me as a part of my life and personality. I remembered my time there vividly. It shaped me as a journalist and as a person. When I heard there were American fathers going back to get their Vietnamese children out of Vietnam, I knew I had to do the story. I always knew about the children of G.I.s who had been left behind. Their fathers either couldn't take them to the U.S. because of American policy, or had simply left them. And these children, abandoned by their dads for whatever reason, were not accepted into Vietnamese society. In fact, they were often rejected. The Vietnamese called them, poetically, "Children of the Dust." They were the ones left over after the American occupation.

Not only was I going to do the story, but I was going to make a documentary on the subject. I convinced my bosses at ARD that we had do the story. Once they gave their blessing, I was on my way back to Vietnam. It was the end of the 1980s. This was still in Bush's term, and I was returning to the country for the first time in nearly two decades.

The plane landed at Tan Son Nhat Airport without difficulty. There was no gunfire, and not a single mortar fell. I can't say that I was disappointed, but you get used to a place under certain conditions. For me, Saigon and the airport had always been under siege.

So much had changed since the early '70s. First, it was no longer Saigon. It was named Ho Chi Minh City. But I refused to call it anything other than Saigon. They even renamed the streets, which was a more difficult change to fight. If you said Saigon, people might not agree with you, but at least they knew what you were talking about. After fifteen years people had forgotten the old names of streets, or never knew they were changed at all. And the food was so different, too, but for the better. The food actually had fresh spices in it now. You didn't realize how the war had hurt their farming. Saigon was so isolated by the fighting that all the wonderful flavors disappeared from the Vietnamese menu during the war. We thought that this was how the food tasted—somewhat bland—but now everything we ate was full of spices I never realized they used. I had their national dish, pho soup, and the difference in taste was drastic. I tasted this soup at more than one location, not just the hotel, so it wasn't simply a matter of one chef's recipe over another's.

We stayed at the Majestic Hotel on the Saigon River. Apparently, they didn't think to change the name of the river as well. The Continental Hotel was under renovations at that time, so we couldn't stay there. The Majestic was a fine hotel. It was where American officers stayed during the war. But I wasn't interested in our accommodations. I wanted to meet the children of the G.I.s and tell their stories.

We met our guide in the hotel lobby. We planned to travel north on Highway 1 up to Qui Nhon. Our guide for the trip, it turned out, was a Vietcong soldier who had fought in the Mekong Delta during the war. Now he was taking us to a nice restaurant before we left the city. Sure enough, we got into a discussion.

I called the city Saigon.

"When will we leave Saigon? Saigon looks much different from how I remembered it."

He shrugged it off. I think there was an effort by the Vietnamese to ease relations with the United States, and maybe his easy attitude was part of it. But when we raised the topic of finding the G.I.s' children, who were no longer children by then, he began to give his opinion on the war. He talked about how the Americans had committed many atrocities during that time.

By then, my crew was obviously becoming a little uncomfortable with what was happening between the guide and me. They didn't want me to argue with him. We had come all this way to make a film. But I didn't want to let what he said go.

"In the Delta, I saw groups of children chained together with a rifle so they couldn't run away. They had to shoot at the Americans to cover the Vietcong's escape."

"People did bad things," he said.

"I saw this several times, and I know that it happened many other times. This was more than just some bad people: this was policy. You must have seen it, too. The Americans would never have done anything like that, not as a policy."

"We are trying to put the war behind us," he said.

My crew was tense. They wanted me to stop. I had said what I wanted, so I stopped, but I didn't like him telling me the Americans were just as ruthless as the Vietcong because they weren't. I had seen it.

We soon left for Qui Nhon. I had never driven around Vietnam before. Even when we left Saigon for the coast and R&R, we took a helicopter, not a Jeep. One of the only times I took a Jeep, we encountered gunfire from the hillsides after we had assumed the road was clear. But now our journey north wasn't easy, either. The road was still full of bomb craters. They had not fixed them after all these years, and several bridges were still out. Our van had to drive precariously over timbers covering the old bridge foundations. It took us the entire day to go a distance that in Germany would take only four hours.

In Qui Nhon, the American G.I. who we were filming met with his daughter. Her mother's family had taken care of her all these years, and now her father was here to take her to the States. The American had two children by the same woman. When the war ended, he somehow was able to get his wife and their other children out of the country, but they were not allowed to take this child. Now he had come to get her once and for all, but he was stopped. She cried terribly. He had come all this way for her, and the Vietnamese would not let her go.

The problem, in many instances, was twofold. Not only had the State Department been very reluctant to take the families of G.I.s back into the States, but the Vietnamese would not let them go, either. Especially with children, if an American couldn't prove through documentation that the child was his, then he couldn't take his child back to America. There was still bitterness between the two countries, and it played out here among other places.

The child, who was denied permission to leave while we were there, was later allowed to move to the States with her family. Many were not so fortunate, nor did they have a family to take care of them in Vietnam. In these cases, they lived in the streets. They were shunned because they were the children of Americans—"Children of the Dust"—and were in a terrible kind of limbo as pawns between two adversarial governments.

While we were discussing our film and the places we wanted to shoot, I suddenly had a great idea.

"You know, I could use some Vietnamese music for the opening of the documentary." When I told our guide about the opening scenes, he immediately said, "We can compose something so it could fit."

"How much?"

"Five hundred dollars," he responded. I gave him the money. He said that when he was finished, he would drop off the piece for me at the German Embassy in Hanoi. I was a little skeptical but thought it would be a coup if it worked. I believed him. I had gotten to know the Vietnamese while I was there, and he seemed like a man you could trust. But as soon as I got back from Vietnam, I told my Bureau Chief, "I think I lost ARD $500 for music they were going to compose and play for the documentary." He wasn't upset.

A few weeks later, to my surprise, I got a package in the mail at ARD. It was an audiocassette with the music. As he promised, the guide had it made and delivered it to the German Embassy in Hanoi. They, in turn, sent it to our Bonn office, which sent it to the German Embassy in Washington, who sent it to our office. I had written the thing off. They actually had composed music for the video based on some specifications I had given to our guide. And they gave it to me in several versions: a traditional Vietnamese version, a modern version, and a jazz version. And all in time to make the editing process and the final cut.

CHAPTER 26

Birthdays

I was at Benihana of Tokyo for dinner with my son Peter and my daughter Petra. The Japanese steakhouse was our favorite restaurant. I was divorced from Dick by then, and he was not with us but called on the phone. Someone from the restaurant came and got me.

"Mrs. Rosenbaum, you have a phone call." We were in the middle of dinner. I left the table and took the call.

"What happened?" I answered, knowing Dick wouldn't call us at a restaurant if it wasn't important.

"Sorry, but two of our F-14 Tomcats shot down two Libyan Sukhois. The Libyan planes fired at the Tomcats during a U.S. naval exercise off Libya's coast." Dick explained that this little air war might have consequences, and everybody was on high alert.

It was August 19th, 1981, and Muammar Gaddafi, a known terrorist, had been a thorn in the side of the Reagan administration since his inauguration. Reagan had taken action right after being sworn into office. He decreed that any U.S. plane being targeted could return fire immediately.

I walked back over to the table where Petra and Peter were waiting. "I'm sorry, but you have to eat quickly. We have to go to the office." This may sound odd, or maybe mean, but my kids had come with me before when these kinds of events occurred. They knew the drill. They finished eating, and I drove over to our Washington D.C. offices. Neither Peter nor Petra complained. Of course, you could say I was married to ARD, which I was, but I was fortunate in my occupation and in my position because Peter and Petra could sometimes actually participate in what I did. Not only that, but they even seemed to like it.

I had to leave them often, and we made sacrifices, but there were also some unique perks that we all got to enjoy. When Petra was older, I took her to Disney World when I produced a story there. Petra got to go to any of the parks while we were working. She chose the Magic Kingdom, her favorite one since she was four. She was also a huge help to me because she was culturally American, and I wasn't, so she knew whom we should be filming and whom we should ignore.

The night when Reagan struck Libya, we got into the office, and Petra said, "Mom, I'll do the telephones." And Peter, then twelve, immediately volunteered to tape everything coming in on television and log the material. We had a deal where we could reuse the footage from the American networks in Germany. Both my kids knew how to use the recording machines since an early age. I even had a machine at home, which was cabled into the TV. One night I was running late at the office. I called the house to let the sitter know. Petra answered the phone. When I told her I would be late, she didn't cry or complain but just said, "Do you want me to tape ABC news?"

"Yes."

"I can tape CBS, too, if you want?"

"Okay, that will be great."

She was only four years old. I thought, "What great kids I have."

So that night after Benihana, the kids knew what to do when we walked into the office at ARD. Peter knew exactly where to go for the taping, and Petra knew exactly which buttons to push to receive and connect a call. The Rosenbaum family had the situation well in hand. It was the weekend, and nobody was in the office. My children manned their stations throughout the office, and when our Bureau Chief, Fritz, came in, we didn't skip a beat. He wasn't shocked at what we were doing; he had seen it before, but he was certainly surprised to see two children and their mother at desks, running the office while the others were out and keeping everyone abreast of the story as it happened. The kids had a way of sounding so official. They were like children in oversized adult clothes, working a real job and taking it very seriously. Though they may have looked cute and absurd, they weren't bad at their jobs.

My children were great. I had to be away so often that I sometimes felt they were just born that way, and I was lucky to have them.

One time, Peter saved his sister's birthday. It was my entire fault, of course. I made a mistake because of work. But Peter had a plan, and he was the voice of reason.

It began when Fritz and I decided to do a live show with broadcasts from all over the U.S. This was difficult enough to choreograph with all the possibilities for technical troubles, but on top of that, the program was to be beamed to Germany, which only added to the complications and problems. Fritz and I always wanted to try new things. And we weren't afraid of taking chances.

The broadcast was set to air on February the 26th. Petra's birthday was the day before. This was good since there was no conflict. The show would be coming down to the wire, but I would still have time to take her out for her birthday. I got tickets for a children's theater in D.C. for a group of kids on the afternoon of the 25th. Everything was ready to go.

The day came, and I went around and picked up all the children to take them to the theater. Everyone was happy—Petra most of all. She had all her little friends together and her older brother to accompany her to the theater. When we arrived, they didn't have my reservation.

"Look, you have to have it. I made a reservation for today."

"I'm very sorry, but we don't have it in our book. Your name is not here. Please let me look into this." She looked and found that I had a reservation after all, but I had made it for the 26th. That was D-Day for my ARD production, but it had nothing to do with my daughter. It was a Freudian slip. The date weighed so heavily on my mind that I just scheduled her party for that day without thinking.

Petra was very upset with me. I had all these children who couldn't go to the show because we had no reservation. I felt a mixture of guilt and anger.

"Mom, my birthday is on the 25th," Petra said.

"I know that, it's just . . ." But how do you explain this to a child whose party you've just ruined?

That's when Peter looked at me and said, "Don't worry, we'll just go bowling instead." That seemed to settle the air. Petra no longer focused on the fact that I had ruined her birthday. She must not have been wedded to the idea of going to the theater because she didn't protest the bowling alley. When February rolled around, or even in January, Petra would say, "Mom, don't forget my birthday is on the 25th this year, not the 26th." This lasted for years.

The toll of my job was more than just the time it took me away from my family. It also drew my mind away to the point of interrupting a birthday. But I loved my job, and I had to work. I didn't have the luxury of not working, and if I wanted to maintain the position I loved so much, this was what I had to endure. I suppose I could have pulled back, but I still would have to work, and then probably at a job I didn't like as much.

The ARD live show was a complete failure. I had put together correspondents to report live on various stories from locations all over the United States. We had a satellite link to Germany through a CBS affiliate. The show was all set to go and was the culmination of months of planning between Fritz and me. When the 26th arrived, everything that could go wrong went wrong. "USA Today" also served as a screening for what we hoped would become a monthly program at ARD German Television. That's if all went well. But when the program started, there was just a black screen. We were broadcasting it back to Germany, and something had gone wrong someplace in between.

On the German end, a producer jumped before a camera and said, "Please bear with us. We are having technical difficulties." Within minutes, the show came back on. But only for a few minutes more. Then there was another technical problem, then another and another. Some of the tapes were even miscued. All the way from start to finish, the program went on and off, sometimes for over ten minutes. Then it was over. It was a disaster.

The next morning, Fritz came in with flowers for me. "Well, we'll never do that again," he said. He was right. We could never rely on the fact that our broadcast would work as we hoped it would. We needed a Plan B at all times, in case the satellites failed or there was a human technical error. The bottom line was that we had to be ready with a local backup.

Our editor-in-chief called from Cologne, Germany, and basically yelled at us. You just can't have a major broadcast fail to air all across the country and leave long breaks of black screen. That was nearly unforgivable, though the show did run monthly afterward.

However, one person found humor in the affair. While we were sifting through letters and reviews that came in after the show aired (or failed to air), Fritz told me about a letter to our president.

"I think this is from your father," he said, reading it aloud.

"I have never experienced a more exciting program on your network than the "USA Today" program that aired the other night because you never knew what was going to happen from one moment to the next." It was signed Fritz Krieger. It was my father. I thought, who else would have written such a thing? This was his kind of humor.

I called my dad and told him, "That letter you wrote to ARD was very funny." He just laughed. I'm sure he laughed when he wrote it as well.

But there often wasn't much to laugh at. This was a tough business—a cutthroat business. I often was afraid I would lose my job, especially because I had children. I had to draw the line very carefully between work and my family. When Petra had a severe ear infection, and nosebleed because of it, I stayed with her. There was no other option. You couldn't always go to work, no matter how ambitious you were. In times like these, I was afraid I would get fired. I was afraid not only because we needed the income but because I loved what I did. I loved the challenge and the difficulty of the job, and I loved that I was good at it.

One day, I mentioned the difficulty of having to juggle my career and my kids to a male co-worker. He just looked at me and said, "Your family is your own private affair. Don't bring it to the office." I thought that was such a cruel thing for someone to say. I can't imagine he would have said that to a male co-worker who had to take his daughter to the hospital. But he was also upset I was the producer. I know there were many people who thought I made them do more than they should. For example, I had them arrive at the White House before everyone else, so they would be in a good position to get the best footage. The White House reserved positions for the U.S. networks. For the rest, however, it meant first come, first serve.

We had to fend for ourselves. In that way, the network was very much like me. When I was younger, no one cared if I got a story or not. In fact, many seemed to work against me. I was on my own. That was fine. I knew I had to fight for it. That's how it was with ARD in America. We were fine as long as we fought for it.

And with me as producer, you can bet we fought. The job was not only stressful and hard; it was also exciting and fun. Hey, I got to meet Michael Jackson at the White House. Even my kids thought that was exciting. "Did he wear his famous glove?" they asked. "Yes, he did." Interviewing Muhammad Ali in Las Vegas was really fun, too. The world-famous boxer certainly had charisma. The accident at the atomic plant on Three Mile Island, Pennsylvania, was a logistical nightmare and demanded a level head to cover the story. I rented a Lear Jet, which took us early every morning to Harrisburg.

We left at six o'clock in the morning with our Geiger counters ready to reveal any radiation leakage from the plant. The entrance to the plant was overcrowded with media waiting for a few briefings and interviewing any citizen who lived in the area. It was usually a real madhouse. Diane Sawyer, now a famous anchorwoman, worked for CBS at the time and usually arrived late, so whenever a briefer finished his spiel, Diane would ask, "Can you repeat that for CBS, please?" I always wondered what would happen if I said to a briefer, "Can you repeat that for ARD, please?"

I always strived to be the first and the best. Take, for example, our preparations for the last Iraq war. My bureau chief, Tom Buhrow, and I constantly came up with new toys we could introduce to our viewers. If CNN had a screenwriter, we at ARD had to have one, too, so our own military experts could move divisions with their fingertips and light up the screen with planes and exciting new military moves.

Of course, we had a satellite picture of Baghdad and an expert interpreter. Oh yes, we definitely wanted to pee with the big dog network, and Thea was in seventh heaven. When the war started early by mistake, it was my Washington studio that ran our network's war coverage for an hour and a half, before the main offices in Germany were fully staffed. It was in the middle of the night, but we were prepared. Those were the real highlights of my career, and the more stress, the better.

Yet sometimes I ask myself, "Was it more important to meet every president since Nixon or to spend time with my family?" It can be difficult to choose between meeting historically important people and taking care of your children. But would I do it again? You bet I would.

Epilogue

I was sitting in Senator Nelson's Fort Myers office. Rana Erbrick, a city council woman in Cape Coral, and friend suggested I come here. I applied for my United States citizenship in January 2013, but month after month passed, and I couldn't get a word from immigration on what was going on. I had been fingerprinted back in February. After that, it was only supposed to be a month and a half before I got my interview, but it never happened. Now I was here to ask for help. I hoped that at least I could get Senator Nelson's office to write a letter on my behalf.

It worked. About a week later, Homeland Security advised me of my interview date. A day after that, Senator Nelson's office sent me a confirmation letter, along with a copy of a letter from immigration, apologizing for the delay. "Well," I thought, "That's the magic of a Senator's office. Thank you, Senator Nelson!"

I was happy because the wait was over and I would be a citizen, which I never thought I would become. When I married Dick in 1963, we came back to the States, where I met his mother in Overland Park, Kansas. She greeted me, saying, "Now you can become a citizen," as if my motivation for marrying her son was to become an American. When I heard those words, I thought: "If she thinks that, then I'll never become a citizen." And I never did.

In the early years of my stay in America, I didn't become one because I wouldn't let his mother be right, even in her own mind, about my motives for marrying my husband. But as time passed and I became a Senior Producer for ARD German television, I refrained from getting American citizenship even though I spent most of my time in the States. The producer for German television should at least have the good grace to remain German.

I retired from that position in 2005 and moved with my husband, Jens, to Florida. Jens died soon after our move. What was I to do? I had lived in the United States off and on for almost fifty years. By then, there was no real reason why I shouldn't become an American. I couldn't nurse a grudge forever, and I no longer worked as a German TV producer. Why not get my citizenship? But that wasn't very motivating.

What finally motivated me was the realization that I was already an American and always had been. The country is a melting pot. Everyone is from somewhere else. I was a German, but even my early reporting was in an American style, and my producing was a translation of American to German.

My story is undoubtedly an American one. I was an immigrant who had come here to seek a better future and found it. I was also a part of a country that had a strangely American story. In a profound and large-scale way, the recent history of West Germany and West Berlin was an American story. Just as my story would not have been possible without America, West Germany and the German reunification would not have been possible without America.

I was sworn in as a United States citizen on August 13, 2013, to the cheers of my friends and the rest of the small audience assembled there that day. I was surrounded by new Americans from as many as thirty different countries. These people had likely been Americans for their entire lives, but on that day, they made it official. We exchanged glances, knowing we'd never see one another again, but that we had just done something very important together. We were looking at one another with both congratulations and a curiosity for what each of us would do from here.

At least for me, now that it's official, I think I'll do some reporting. However, I won't be reporting from places like Khe Sanh, Honduras, Iraq, or future counterparts, regardless of how exciting that might be. I think local politics might be more my speed for the time being. Of course, I have a connection with Senator Nelson's office.